Souls magnified

8/99

Tom + Barb —

this is a collection of
sermons — stories,
really — by an
expansive soul who is
at once open +
immersed in life's
journey yet keenly
aware of the process
she is experiencing. Her
joy in + appreciation of
life resonates in me —
as do both of you
wonderful people + dear
friends — B.

Also by Gretchen Thompson

(Under the name G. F. Thompson)

Slow Miracles: Urban Women Fighting for Liberation

Souls magnified

a book of sermons

Gretchen Thompson

Minneapolis • Bright Feather Press • 1998

On the cover: After a fire in the sanctuary of Unity-Unitarian Church, St. Paul, Minnesota, in the 1960s, the congregation turned the hole burnt in the roof into this skylight and added a reredos sculpted in wood.

Cover photo: J. Quinn Campbell, St. Paul
Editing/design: E. B. Green Editorial, St. Paul
Printing: Sexton Printing, Inc., St. Paul
Binding: Muscle Bound Bindery, Minneapolis

For additional copies of this publication, write:
Bright Feather Press
P.O. Box 19425
Minneapolis, MN 55419

Contents

To

William R. Anderson, Jr.,

in loving remembrance

Foreword

As we look back on the 20th century, we remember many great souls—Mother Teresa, Nelson Mandela, and Elie Wiesel are three—who have accomplished magnificent deeds for humanity. But for our true heroes and heroines, we must look for great souls—the ones who give more than they take, who provide inspiration, insight and strength—in our midst.

During the past three years, the congregation of a Unitarian church in St. Paul, Minnesota, has been blessed with the preaching gifts of such an extraordinary soul. From the first time I heard Gretchen Thompson, I have looked with awe on her ability to speak from a living inner reality, out of a vibrant, luminous source of deep vitality. Her sermons reveal an understanding of pain, suffering and sacrifice, making way always to the blossoming of new life. Some congregants have spoken of her as a talented storyteller, others of her warmth of heart. I find her to have deep and expansive qualities of soul.

While homilies set in type can never duplicate Gretchen's delivery in person, requests for a collection of her sermons have nevertheless poured forth. You will learn in this volume of ten that Gretchen Thompson has the rare ability both to find a true inner space that comes from her experience in the world and to speak from it. Her inner experience becomes word, becomes flesh, and dwells among us. And you will be able to draw from these words her deep insight and joy.

—BILL MANNING

A sermon is a communal event, neither created nor spoken in isolation. At its best, it issues first from the soul of a gathered people, springs into the heart of a preacher, mingles there with prayer, deep thought and sacred word from all ages, sometimes even tears things up a little, and then comes out again rounded and beautiful, like a gift appreciated and used, now returned to its original owner.

At its best, it magnifies the souls—dilates the holiness—of all concerned: the congregation, the preacher, then all the gathered worshippers—congregants and guests.

First, then, I thank the people of Unity Church–Unitarian in St. Paul, Minnesota, whose presence during these past three years has given life to so many of my sermons.

Also, I thank Ellen Green, a gifted and compassionate editor and designer; John O'Brien, whose artistic sensitivities regarding sermon selection have proven invaluable; Mary Anderson, whose generosity of spirit makes so much possible; and Quinn Campbell, whose fine photography graces the cover of this volume and brings me much joy.

—GRETCHEN THOMPSON

Souls magnified

And Mary said, My soul doth magnify the Lord, and my spirit hath rejoiced in God my Savior. For he hath regarded the low estate of his handmaiden: for, behold, henceforth all generations shall call me blessed.—*Luke 1:46–48*

It was his own room . . . but it had undergone a surprising transformation. The walls and ceiling were so hung with living green, that it looked a perfect grove, from every part of which, bright, gleaming berries glistened . . .

Heaped up upon the floor, to form a kind of throne, were turkeys, geese, game, poultry, brawn, great joints of meat, suckling pigs, long wreathes of sausages, mince pies, plum puddings, barrels of oysters, red-hot chestnuts, cherry-cheeked apples, juicy oranges, luscious pears, immense twelfth-cakes, and seething bowls of punch, that made the chamber dim with their delicious steam. In easy state upon this couch, there sat a jolly Giant, glorious to see; who bore a glowing torch, in shape not unlike Plenty's horn, and held it up, high up, to shed its light on Scrooge, as he came peeping round the door.

"Come in!" exclaimed the Ghost. "Come in, and know me better, man . . . I am the Ghost of Christmas Present . . ."

"Spirit," said Scrooge submissively, "conduct me where you will . . ."

And perhaps it was the pleasure the good Spirit had in showing off this power of his, or else it was his own kind, generous hearty nature, and his sympathy with all poor men, that led him straight to Scrooge's clerk's; for there he went, and took Scrooge with him, holding to his robe; and on the threshold of the door the Spirit smiled, and stopped to bless Bob Cratchit's dwelling with the sprinklings of his torch . . .

Then up rose Mrs. Cratchit, dressed out but poorly in a twice-turned gown, but brave in ribbons, which are cheap, and make a goodly show for sixpence . . . And now two smaller Cratchits, boy and girl, came tearing in, screaming that outside the baker's they had smelt the goose, and known it for their own; and basking in luxurious thoughts of sage and onion, these young Cratchits danced about the table . . .

Tiny Tim sat very close to his father's side, upon his little stool. Bob held his withered little hand in his, as if he loved the child, and wished to keep him by his side; and dreaded he might be taken from him.

"Spirit," said Scrooge, with an interest he had never felt before, "tell me, if Tiny Tim will live."

"I see a vacant seat," replied the Ghost . . .

"No, no," said Scrooge. "Oh no, kind Spirit, say he will be spared."

"If he be like to die, he had better do it, and decrease the population."

Scrooge hung his head to hear his own words quoted by the Spirit, and was overcome with penitence and grief.

—*Charles Dickens*

The Magnificat, famous now and set in music so beautiful —the Magnificat, taken from Luke, from the deep and ancient story, the words of a young woman pregnant with possibility—these words, this text, once meant little to me.

I imagined the young woman, Mary, face calm and pure, linen cloth draped gracefully across her brow, perhaps a hint of light glowing round her countenance. Calm, like a porcelain figure in a crèche. Poor, yes, but the barn would be cozy. Outcast, yes, but that was just part of the story, and what did it really mean, anyway?

Then, when I was in seminary, something happened that allowed me to hear the Magnificat differently.

There was a woman whose physical disability caused her to have frequent muscle spasms in arms and legs and face, to the extent that she found it difficult to walk and handle books, difficult to talk. I don't know what the formal diagnosis was; that is not relevant. I found myself wondering, though, how she would ever be a parish minister. Even if she were brilliant academically, deeply compassionate, wise—how would a congregation ever come to see past her physical self to the whole person she was?

I admired her courage, her going to seminary. And I noticed early on that she was intelligent and compassionate. But to be honest, I found it hard to look at her, to be with her, to be in conversation with her. I didn't know why. Something about her made me uncomfortable.

It was advent, this time of year, the time of waiting in expectation. We were preparing for a worship service that would include the words from Luke, the ancient words of the Magnificat.

This woman, this disabled woman, said, with quiet authority, "I would like to play the part of Mary."

I could imagine she had never been allowed to be Mary in an Advent or Christmas event before. Of course, they would pick— it would be human nature to pick—a little girl who instead looked serene, like the gentle Mary in the crèche, one who looked beautiful, calm, and spiritually peaceful. Not a little one whose arms and legs kept shooting out, who kept making distracting noises. That one never would have been picked.

Now here she was, a grown woman, claiming that position.

The day of the service came, and we were all in our places. The lights in the sanctuary were dim. She entered, fully dressed as Mary. She wore the long, flowing white robe with gold trim, moved in an unpredictable way to a space near the altar. On her head was the draped stole that so classically marks the mother of Jesus in all the scenes and pictures, on all the cards. It was very crooked.

But when this woman began to speak the Magnificat, I heard it in a way I had never heard it before. And she changed my understanding of its meaning profoundly, to the bone.

Not just, "My soul magnifies the Lord . . ."

"*My* soul doth magnify the Lord," she began. Meaning not just the souls of the beautiful-seeming ones, of the serene-seeming ones, the ones in the crèches, who have no pain, no flaws. No. My soul—too—magnifies the Lord. I—too—am pregnant with the possibility of holiness. My own, strange-seeming body is the site of the miracle. Here. Now.

She went on. "*My* spirit rejoiceth in God my Savior, who hath looked with favor on the lowliness of his servant." Meaning yes, my uniqueness is manifest; there is no secret about it. I don't even try to hide it because with this configuration of physical challenges I cannot hide it. Yet even so, the Miracle is upon me and dwells within me. I am a child of this universe. I belong here.

The words of the holy poem followed from her one on the other—erratic, punctuated with muscle jerks and spasmodic noises. When she was done, a long silence held in the sanctuary. All of us—seminary students, professors, those by vocation dedicated to grapple with the Mystery—were impregnated with something new and powerful and frightening.

I never spoke to anyone else about it. But I could no longer turn away from her, or forget her, or pretend she was not there. And I knew why she frightened me. In looking at her, I was seeing some version of myself.

Her eccentricities, her struggles, her challenges, were on the outside—in the very appearance and nature of her body. She could not hide them; they were always apparent to the world.

Mine, by contrast, were more internal, though no less real. My eccentricities, struggles, challenges were inside of me. I could hide them if I chose. But that didn't mean I was without them or would ever be.

And her message to me—that her soul, mine, the human soul, the flawed, struggling, pain-knowing, human soul—was indeed a magnification, a making larger upon the earth, or a making incarnate, of the soul of God. Not just if we don't seem deformed, not just if we do it right—earn enough money, are kind enough to strangers, give enough away, succeed enough, or raise well-mannered and well-educated children. Not just if, but as we are.

At Unity Church, we speak of the divine seed, the deep holiness, within each human being. In what culture, in what context, in what ferment, does seed grow? Will it grow on silver platters? Or in crystal bowls? In a porcelain crèche? Will it grow in any place sterile? Or perfect-seeming? Or reft of complexity?

No. Seeds grow in the dirt, in the complex, roiling mix of transforming, decaying, breaking down, and building life forces, wet and then dry as bone, cracking, freezing, fecund, motley, messy, crumbling, earth. Not perfect. Not pure or pristine. Seeds grow in dirt.

We have this idea that we must be something, put some thing forward, some thing that looks and seems and is exceptional, more perfect than we are. And inside, countless numbers of us experience something far more complex—a turbulent mix of roiling transformation, living and dying, fecundity, pebbles, sticks, grains of sand, dead animals, moisture, seed explosion, and on and on. We are grieving those we've lost and struggling with long and old troubles. We are remembering and wishing. We are embroiled in loneliness and discouragement, worried about no end of things.

And we are celebrating and singing, spilling things on our best clothes, laughing in the daytime, and weeping in the night. We are selfish one day, generous the next, angry at children, then at ourselves, trying so often to make it look the way it is not. It is not simple. And it is not serene like the crèche.

And yet I would posit, even as it is, it is holy. It is holy that a poor woman, deemed inferior before the whole world by virtue of both gender and class, carried within her a Christ child. It is holy that we—with all our strange exterior, our interior flaws and eccentricities, with all our complex passions and pains and impulses to rejoice and to curse one another—it is holy that we dare to hope that divine seed lives within us. It is holy that divinity struggles to emerge from the humble soil of our real selves, that we don't have to be perfect, that we are made of the earth.

I don't know what happened to that woman in the seminary. I myself, entering the ordained ministry, went on to learn about something that happens unfailingly at this time of year to those in my role, that all kinds of people turn up asking for all kinds of things.

I don't mean congregants coming to visit with questions, or concerns. I mean strangers, needful strangers.

"Are you by chance the pastor? Listen, I got a flat tire on my way to my first job, I'm gonna be late, can you spare a ten? I'll give it back at the first paycheck. Promise."

"Say, are you the pastor? My wife's at home with the new baby, but we're out of diapers. Can you give me some cash?"

"Excuse me, Pastor," (seems they always call me pastor) "but my grandkids got dumped off at my place, and they're going hungry. Can you help? I just want to buy them some oatmeal and some canned fruit."

One learns that many of these requests are scams and, in these days, often related to the purchase of drugs or alcohol. And that nobody ever pays you back. After a while, you can develop this attitude where you just say no . . . no . . . no. And perhaps that is the way it should be.

Once, a man named Quincy Smith came and asked me for money. He was the tenth, maybe the fifteenth one, that year.

"No," I said. "Sorry, friend." And to myself, "You've got bad news written all over your face. And I hope to God the story about the wife and kids is a bald-faced lie because I hate to think of anyone waiting at home for you to come through for them."

Dirt. Earth. Humus.

I had problems of my own. But he came back three times. Why was he picking on me? Did I look like a sucker, or what?

Why was he making me so uncomfortable? I didn't even notice, then, that I didn't like to look at him. It should have been a sign.

The third time he came, I was angry. "I tell you, Mr. Smith, I don't give out handouts, I just don't do it. So you can forget it. You can stop coming here. It's not going to work!"

"Do you ever hire folks?"

"Why? Why do you ask? What can you do?"

"I play music, Pastor."

"You play music." I was impatient, doubtful. "And what do you play?"

"Mouth harp, Pastor."

"Look, quit calling me pastor. And I wouldn't even consider hiring you without listening to you first, so let's go to the sanctuary right now."

And we did. And he played, on his mouth harp, a strange, jazzy, pain-filled, distinctly imperfect but very soulful version of "Silent Night."

"Quincy Smith, I like the way you play. You're hired. Christmas Day, be here at 10:00 A.M. I'll pay you fifty bucks. Don't let me down."

"How 'bout a cash advance?"

"No."

At the time, it just seemed like nothing, nothing. But it wasn't nothing. It was something, something important happening, for him, and for me. It was two flawed souls, magnifying something far more mysterious than either could comprehend.

Christmas Day there I was, all dressed up, trying to put what I thought was my best self forward. I knew what that crèche looked like. I knew how it was supposed to be, how I was supposed to come across. I really didn't expect Quincy Smith to come, had a piano solo all figured out for backup.

But at 9:45 A.M. in he comes with two tough-looking guys alongside him, one on the right, one on the left. Same clothes he's always had on, but this time with a Santa hat jaunty on top, and a pair of gigantic sunglasses.

"You Pastor Thompson?" one of the guys says.

"Yes, I am. Who are you?"

"I'm so-and-so from so-and-so treatment center. Mr. Smith here was arrested a while back on such-and-such a charge, but because he's got some addiction issues, he opted to go to treatment instead of jail. He tells us that he has a gig here this morning, and so we brought him over. Sorry, ma'am, we can't let him out of our sight. But he's here to play, and he's agreed to go straight from here to his house to drop off the cash for his wife and kids."

Jesus Christ.

I looked into his eyes, and there I was, a partner to someone, not always a very good one; a parent to someone, who got angry too often and forgot to be tender. A musician, an addict, a liar, a cripple like Tiny Tim, a cripple like Scrooge—a soul. A failure and a success, a soul magnified, a dirty, clean, all-dressed-up dressed-down soul.

"Well, I'll be damned," I said. "Merry Christmas. Let's do it."

And we did. Those two guys sat in the front row the whole time. I still wonder whether the congregation thought I'd brought in bouncers that day. And Quincy Smith, whoever he really was, played "Silent Night" on his mouth harp, and took his fifty dollars, and wandered off escorted by the law into his crazy corner of the cosmos, leaving me dumbfounded in mine.

I have come to believe that you and I and Quincy Smith and the one who spoke the Magnificat and Scrooge and Tiny Tim Cratchit and the president and the pope are all like that, all the same. All of us magnify the soul of the Lord—uniquely and imperfectly, like divine seeds growing in the dirt.

The task—the religious task, by no means an easy one—is to live into the magnification, the magnificence, rather than away from it, to keep our eyes open to it, instead of closing them in fear or distaste or disdain.

It is just so much easier to pretend that the world is a porcelain crèche. That, I believe, is what most of us do most of the time, as we arrange our houses and our lives and our expectations. We engage with one another so carefully, and we hide what hurts, so as to put forward to the world what we think will impress. And we don't tell people about the real stuff—the complexity of our own profound earthiness, which embraces and sustains the miracle of our own divinity like a loamy, rocky cradle.

The Ghost, that night, took Scrooge to the far ends of the earth, showing him poverty and suffering such as he had never before witnessed. The Ghost journeyed with him until he had gained wisdom, until he had gained deep compassion, and until he had gained reverence for the holiness of all life:

> It was a long night, if it was only a night . . . It was strange, too, that while Scrooge remained unaltered in his outward form, the Ghost grew older, clearly older . . .
>
> The bell struck twelve. Scrooge looked about him for the Ghost, and saw it not.

—December 15, 1996

Sandlot religion

We dare not fence the spirit.—*Wallace Robbins*

One of the most endearing qualities of baseball is its role in the human imagination.—*Joel Zoss and John Bowman*

Religion, in one sense, is like baseball or any other form of play or art. The professionals who play in the big leagues render a great service to our culture. Baseball would certainly not pervade our national life as it does if it were not for these big leagues. But if you want to find out the true spirit of baseball in all the glory of a passion, you must not go to the big leagues. You must go to the backyard, the sandlot, the side street, and the school ground. There it is not a profession, it is a passion. This is as true of religion as it is of baseball. Among the professionals you find superb mastery and a great technique, but not too frequently the pure devotion. Perhaps in baseball the passion is not too important, but in religion it is all-important. A religion that is not passionate simply is not worth considering. Therefore, I say, we need more sandlot religion. The professional, whether White Sox or Methodist, controls inordinately our baseball and our religion.
—*Henry Nelson Wieman*

Funny, I'm still not sure whether this is a sermon about baseball or a sermon about religion.

When I was in college, Tom Ferguson, the man who eventually would become my husband, was known as a superb athlete, an ace pitcher for our school team, powerful at bat. In the spring of the year that we fell in love, he gave me a beautiful, blue baseball mitt—my first mitt ever—so that I too could play in pickup games.

That year was indeed the finest of my entire ball-playing career. I remember especially a late spring ball game in which Carleton English Literature Department faculty members took on their students, Tom and myself included. I had received the blue mitt by then, and so, my courage bolstered somewhat with beer, I volunteered to play—of all positions, shortstop—for the student team.

Something about the day—the warmth, the blue of the sky or the mitt, the desire on my part to outwit those who knew so much more than I about Chaucer and Keats and Joyce, probably the beer, too—caused my eye-hand coordination and my response time to skyrocket. So much so that although Professor Owen Jenkins had on numerous occasions encouraged my writing with both kindness and force, on that day I plucked his line drive out of the sky as though I owed him nothing but trouble. And Professor Phillip Sheridan, who had guided me tenderly through the complex meanings of Spenser, was astounded when

I snatched up his grounder and shot it to first base with perfect accuracy eons before he could reach the bag.

The whole game went like that! My young, sweet husband-to-be, shirtless and speechless at the pitcher's mound, smiled at me as though I were a complete and utter mystery.

Every career has its peak. This was mine.

Never again, for me, was there a day or a game quite like that one. The blue mitt I carried tenderly across the years, through marriage and childbearing, until our boys found it in the back of a closet one summer morning, asked if they could take it, then in innocence lost it somewhere on the playground.

Over time, work and stress and aging took their toll. I played ball less and less frequently, then not at all. These days I'm just a fan, though a passionate one. I sit dreamy at the edge of the high-school field in a folding chair, books stacked beside me, and watch our firstborn son—so like his father long ago—pitch for the school team. I scrunch my eyes shut whenever he gets to a full count. My heart soars with every ball that he slams with his strong, young arms into the deep blue sky. And I think about how this too, lovely as it is, will pass—like the blue mitt or the single game in which I found myself a stellar shortstop.

I don't know much about baseball, really. But Wieman's words about baseball and religion catch me, I believe, because they ring so true. There are two worlds indeed. There's this whole professional world that many of us know so well, by virtue of functioning in it or knowing those who do. It's a world one gets prepared for extensively—schooled for, formally or informally, where one develops true expertise, becomes known and paid for certain skills, masteries, techniques. One suits up for it, often—if not in a baseball uniform, then in a necktie and coat, or earrings and patent leather shoes, or one getup or another.

And when you're in this world, others watch, and determine, your marketability or your value—less according to the depth of your passion, more according to the quality of your performance as compared to the performance of others in your field.

And that's how you end up in either the minors or the majors—depending upon some volatile combination of skill and connection and how hard you're willing to work, how much you're willing to sacrifice. A whole world unto itself is this professional world, with its own importance in the grand scheme of things. I'm not denying that.

But there *is* another world, Wieman says—the world of the sandlot games, the backyard games, the playground—where you don't get paid, and you don't suit up, and you don't get traded and bought and sold, or owned by one team or another.

In the world of the sandlot, your passion counts far more than your competence. The ways you choose to love life and embrace it, the ways you risk and engage, even throw yourself into what you most value, the ways that you live and breathe and have your being in relation to what you care about—these are what count.

Two different worlds, he says. And I can see that both are important and, also, interrelated—inseparable perhaps. Show me a sandlot player who hasn't dreamed, at least once, of what it would be like to be a pro. Or show me a pro who hasn't known, doesn't remember with deep gladness, the sweet passions of the sandlot. Two worlds, related and distinct.

Yet the religious life—the life of the spirit—Wieman says, belongs at heart on the sandlot. Because religion is not, in the end, about quality performance or fame or fortune, or about how successful you become. It's about loving and engaging in life with whole heart and soul, with passion and tenderness and that certain kind of abandon that just does not bow down before performance evaluation or professional expertise.

It's sandlot religion when you dare not fence the spirit but feel compelled instead to let it soar like a fly ball on a spring day, way up towards the deep blue sky, past the bounded edges of fear and expectation—into the Mystery.

In case this hasn't occurred to you, dear congregants, this morning, I might point out that I myself am functioning among you, right now, as a professional. A religious professional, one of your religious professionals, in fact. Look at me, all suited up in this robe and stole.

But I want to tell you something. In my heart of hearts, I'm a sandlot player. If someone were to come to me and say, "Gretchen, you have to pick the one world or the other, the profession or the passion—give up either the day you graduated from seminary or the day you played shortstop for the student team—I would not give up the day I played shortstop and all that day stands for. I couldn't.

So are you, as a body, sandlot players, I believe. I probably wouldn't be here otherwise. Because, except for the intermittent innings that I'm up here in my suit, trying to whack out homers (or at least not strike out), I'm often sitting in a folding chair at the edge of the field, watching you play.

Believe me, from where I sit, your game is really something to behold. There is so much of spirit for me to admire: in your religious lives, in your personal lives, in your work lives.

I know you well enough by now to know that if I go on much longer about how wonderful I think you are, at least some of you will become uncomfortable and tell me that I'm being too sentimental or mushy. But I can't lie, either.

You do come often to speak to me of your lives. I have a pretty good sense of what you struggle with, what you value, and what you seek in your religious lives, your spiritual lives. And you don't speak to me about fame. You don't come speak to me about fortune or any other measures by which the world at large assesses professional expertise.

You come to me to speak about the covenants you have made with others, how hard they are to keep sometimes, how important they are, always.

You talk about the terrors of risk-taking in the name of what you value most, about the unceasing complexity of figuring out what is right and then doing it, about grappling with the difficult distinctions between what you can control and what you cannot, what you must embrace and what you must let go of, about what you find beautiful beyond belief or disturbing beyond comprehension.

Let's face it. We're sandlot players here. We're not going to win the World Series. Our stadium is peculiar at best. I doubt that anybody among us is going to get traded to the White Sox or the Methodists.

We gather here because life has astounded us into playing a game of mythical proportion, and all that we—any of us—would claim as a tool of the trade, is something akin to a blue mitt, or a memory of a blue mitt, or a dream of one. And a rickety fence that doesn't keep spirit in, so that some balls just fly right on past.

And a blue sky, very high, wide open to the Mystery.

—June 14, 1998

Pilgrimage

We shall not cease from exploration
And the end of all our exploring
Will be to arrive at where we started
And know the place for the first time.
                                        —*T. S. Eliot*

How amiable are thy tabernacles, O Lord of hosts!
My soul longeth, yea, even fainteth, for the courts of the
    Lord:
My heart and my flesh crieth out for the living God.
                                        —*Psalm 84:1–2*

S ome journeys outward are also journeys inward, taking us
both far away and towards the very heart of things. Some
journeys forward are also journeys backward, plunging us
simultaneously into uncertain futures and even deeper pasts.
Some journeys have endings embedded in their beginnings and
new beginnings in their endings.

All such journeys defy normalcy. The ways they curve through
time and space and spirit are neither linear nor plain. They bear

tremendous power for transformation. These are journeys to the site of holy ground, the court of the Lord, and therefore called *pilgrimage.*

You have been on at least one, the first one that all of us share and none of us remember, that pilgrimage from the milky, breathless womb out onto the holy ground of this broken, beating earth, moving from a golden fleck of the cosmos, God's wish, into this lifetime, this place.

But there are other pilgrimages—many others—some entirely inexplicable, some more familiar. Like the dizzying passage down the aisle towards the vows of union with another human being. Or the disturbing, mysterious approach to the deathbed of a loved one. Or the return to the site of one's ancestry to stand upon the soil there and breathe and dream and understand anew.

Pilgrimage. We go. We depart from the everyday, we set off up the mountain for holy ground, journey's end, and new beginning. Yet there are other kinds of journeys as well, and we make them every day, rushing here, worrying there, trying to finish this or that.

Which ones are which? How can we know that this stretch, this passage, is pilgrimage, while that other one is something less potent? What marks pilgrimage from the rest?

I believe that there are road signs, signals. The first of these, oddly, is fear. A pilgrimage most often begins with fear. This is as it should be, for true departure from that which is normal or easily understood is never safe. It invites us to change and grow, demands of us that we see new horizons, grasp for new under-standings. It's risky business.

———————

Journal entry for Sunday, October 22, 9:00 A.M. On the plane from Boston to Bangor, Maine, to meet with Arthur Foote, Minister Emeritus of Unity Church–Unitarian:

The woman behind me is weeping with fear as her husband stares ox-eyed out the window.

At least the flight to Boston was slick, glossy. You could almost pretend that nothing was happening. But not now. The tiny silver plane is quaking as though it might explode, jumping like a rabbit. The propellers are grinding and screaming, whipping the cold blue sky to frothy white. You can actually see, down below, the things you'd crash into on impact—cars and people, trees, school buses. It would make a mess, no doubt about that.

The woman sobs even harder, staring right at me, her eyes bright with terror. All of a sudden, oddly, a certain kind of terror strikes me as well. But it is my soul more than my body that lurches, driven off center with doubt. Perhaps her fright-ened eyes triggered it, but no matter, it's mine to deal with now.

What in God's name am I doing here? Six days into a new ministry, hurling through space to the very rim of the con-tinent, to the land of the very roots of this faith tradition in a vehicle made of rubber bands and paper clips, plummeting forward—or is it backward?—through time and space, to meet the history of this congregation head on, in the form of its deeply beloved once-leader. Hurling off for a blessing, with no guarantee it won't be a curse. Because what if Arthur Foote meets me and thinks the fit is all wrong?

It goes on from there, all the fears from recent days and weeks leaping out like ghouls, no everyday ho-hum distractions to keep them locked up—only this blue sky and this sense of impending doom and this wailing woman behind me.

What if this has all been a mistake? What if I never did, still don't, never will belong among these people? What if I fail entirely—on this trip, in this ministry?

Fear and doubt divebomb my gut. Suddenly it seems easier to be the woman with the ox-eyed husband. Or spiraling into a school bus might be more manageable than this.

Who put me on this plane, anyway?

I'm trembling.

Fortunately, fear is not the only signpost that points toward pilgrimage, though it is often the first. What follows fear, more often than not, is longing, deep longing. As the psalmist wrote so long ago, "whose heart and flesh cried out for the living God."

If on our pilgrimages we find some way to be with our fears, don't allow them to derail us, then longing emerges, deep yearning, desire to reach the holy tabernacle for which we first set out. For longing is usually the second signpost, and it will sometimes appear with even more force than the fear that precedes it.

Sometimes a pregnant woman will be so terrified by the initial stages of childbirth that she will literally jump to her feet, screaming, "Let me go! I've changed my mind, I don't want this baby anymore!" *This is fear of pilgrimage.*

Just hours, sometimes minutes later, she will be entirely consumed with the desire to push, to give birth, to hold that same baby in her arms after all. *This is longing for pilgrimage.*

Long-distance runners, I am told, might spend much time before or even well into the start of a race, fretting, feeling profound pain, doubting their ability to finish, and hating the very fact that they have chosen to run at all. *This is fear of pilgrimage.*

Later will come that point—often midrace—where running becomes effortless, blurred, otherworldly, when everything becomes, and stopping becomes unthinkable. *This is longing for pilgrimage.*

Journal from Sunday, October 22, 12:00 noon, between Bangor and Southwest Harbor, pulled over in a rental car:

Good God Almighty! They had all—even the taxi driver in Boston—told me that the leaves would be down, and the trees bare. But the leaves are not down, they are in the trees, in the wind and the sun. Thousands of them, millions, millions of yellow leaves sparking in the bright light along the narrow road. Blinded by their beauty, I can barely see, barely drive.

And yet something in me cannot wait, is compelled down the dazzling road—must get there, must get to the place where the man lives who is beloved, who can tell me the stories as he knew and lived them. That will be holy ground, and I long to get there, long to set my eyes upon his eyes and touch his hand in greeting with my own, outstretched.

It is urgent. He is growing older. Whether he bless or curse me, *I must get there and finish this trip.*

———

First fear, then longing: these are the road signs that a pilgrimage is underway. Perhaps some of you, in your lives right now, are experiencing such road signs. Perhaps you find both terror and desire nudging you along some new, unexplored road and are struggling to find courage to keep going.

Know that neither fear nor longing are at the heart, the core, of such a journey. They have their part, loosening the joints of the soul, preparing us. But they mark our trajectory, not our arrival. And if we are lucky enough to arrive, in some cases if we let ourselves finish, we find ourselves changed—transformed—in ways unimaginable.

Arriving—saying the words of the wedding vow out loud before the gathered people, bidding the loved one in the bed fare-well and deep in our hearts letting go, pushing the baby all the way out—these culminations have the potential to change us so much that when we return, no matter the outcome, all has changed, and we see our old world again, yet for the first time.

Fear, yes. Longing, yes. But the core of any pilgrimage is transformation.

And so we come seeking, seeking the holy, terrified and full of yearning. We come to the tabernacle of the Lord, to the top of the mountain, which could be an ancestral land or the end of a marathon or a deathbed or a wedding dance, or a wise man who may or may not choose to sit and tell the old stories.

———

Journal entry from Tuesday, October 24, 4:00 P.M. On the plane home from visiting Arthur Foote:

Upon arriving Sunday, I called ahead, anticipating that he might be resting. He insisted that I come immediately.

"There is not really very much time," he said into the phone. "Please come now."

And so I went, drove through the blinding bright, golden canopy of leaves, to Arthur Foote, who lives alone now in the home that his deceased wife's ancestors had built upon the ocean more than a century ago.

My heart slams as he ushers me in to sit in the armchair across from his. This is arrival, forward and backward, inward and outward, beginning and ending, a halo around us. sacred space, God's time.

We speak until dark, stopping only for a time of Quaker silence and a bowl of chowder at dusk.

The next day we begin again in the morning, visiting until dark. Arthur teaches me, tells about the old church fire, which for all its destruction did pop out some controversial stained-glass windows and create the gaping hole that became the beautiful sanctuary skylight. He tells a more humorous tale on the side, about his children getting caught building a little fire on the third floor of the parsonage to roast onions.

"Fire seems to be part of my life," he says with a smile.

He answers my questions about his groundbreaking work in mental health reform, and he tells of the week he spent incognito as a staff aide in a mental institution. He describes the shackles, the suffering.

We study hymns together, he holding the new hymnal in his lap, and I the old blue one in mine, the blue one whose creation he spearheaded. We are both too shy to sing.

But he recites poetry, closing his eyes and leaning on his hand. And he asks me many questions and tells about what it is like to throw pots and how he creates the deep blue glaze that is his trademark.

I ask if I might see his old sermon-writing typewriter. "No, too much trouble," he says, "it's upstairs put away in a closet."

We go for a drive, Arthur at the wheel through the bright leaves and the sun. We speak of Rebecca, his spouse and friend and teacher; we speak of Tom, mine. The holiness is not in the words: it hovers around them.

It comes time to go. "Don't bother with a bread-and-butter note," he says.

"But you have given me so much. I don't know if I can help myself."

Then, he says something like, "Wasn't the sun in the leaves blinding, when we went for that drive? I shouldn't have driven, I should have pulled over and let you do it. But I didn't want to."

"I understand. Anyway, I found it blinding, too."

———

Pilgrimage—travel to a holy place—not always easy and so often moving from what is familiar and safe. The plane might crash. The mountain may be too steep. The wise man might say, "No, I have no time for you now." The marriage might fail, its vows giving way. The runner might fall down short of the finish, break bones. There might be pain or confusion or wanting to turn back. But what choice do we have, seeking holy ground?

Back, now, I cannot tell you what has changed, but I know absolutely that something has. It's almost as though I see just the very slightest tinge of golden, that color of sunlight on leaves, in whatever I set eyes upon here, now. It has to do with returning, and seeing for the first time.

I invite you, in your mind's eye, to look. See where you yearn to go, to the place you're supposed to go, not the place where it's easy to go, but the place you long to go, the place where your dreams live. I invite you to see it and believe in it, to return to it always, as though it were both the beginning and the end. It is holy ground and a worthy destination.

—September 22, 1995

Sacred pleasures

My Lord, what a morning!
—*From an American spiritual*

In sorrow shalt thou bring forth children . . . In sorrow shalt
thou eat . . . By the sweat of your brow shalt thou you gain
bread.   —*Genesis 3:16–19*

For love is strong as death . . . and the coals thereof are fire
which hath a most vehement flame. Many waters cannot
quench love, neither can floods drown it.
                                    —*Song of Solomon 8:6–7*

I know one way to get there—to Eden, that is. If you get up
early in the morning, just this time of year, head out across
the Mendota Bridge. Just keep going east and south, and you'll
find an old two-lane road that takes you down through
Wisconsin along the big, rusty train tracks and their sister path,
the sensuous flowing cloud-studded Mississippi.

Then there is a sign marking the place, I can't remember its
name though I wouldn't miss it, to make the turn. You go into

a narrow dirt road arched with trees that are lit up with the early sun, so burning-bright that even the cobwebs seem on fire. At the other end of that is a place, an Eden, so beautiful it seems it must be free of sin or suffering.

What could be more? The corn and the wheat fields, the trees each like a prayer having reached for Heaven, become burdened and lowly with the fruit. The dog with the tattered ear and the white foot nuzzles you curiously as you get out of the car. The stacked bushels and the pastures with the horses, the farmhouse with its wind-beaten porch swing, the morning glories arching up the trellis, throwing off a blue that is steeper and more dizzying than the sea. And all the growing things are right on the edge, ripe to over-ripened, so ragingly alive that they are about to die.

It's all there. The blueberries, the wild daisies, bolted now up from the ground in a last desperate leap for life before snow time; the ferns, backs bent, prepared to simply lie down with dignity. And even the geraniums in pots, the hearty, determined ones, almost to the end, almost gone, their red now turned bruised and purple. And the cloverheads, dark brown knots snarled in the grass, the butterflies hovering, and the cicadas and crickets singing, hymn upon hymn to the end of summer.

And then the white-haired man in the cap, who needs a shave but doesn't really care a whit, comes from the squeaky farmhouse door to give you your basket and instructions.

"Listen, Lady." Gruff, no need to waste words on a morning like this. "Lady. You can pick the Paula Reds. They're over there," he points. "Or pick the Macintoshes, pick the Connell Reds, or the Honey Crisp, the Haralsons. Good pie apples they are, the Haralsons. The Sweet Sixteens, they're something too, and doing fine, just fine this year. But I tell you, those Regents, they're the best damn apples I ever seen. Fine firm flesh, and sweet, well . . . let me tell you Lady, there's nothing like them. But you can't have any 'cause they're not ready yet. Now if you come back in October, maybe they'll be ready for you then. Got it?"

Of course, you get it. It isn't that hard. But walking out through the corn and the wheat fields, past the turning oak and maple, and coming then to the orchard itself, where the smell of apples is heavy and lovely, every single one seeming a gift shaped by God's own hand, every single one a source of pleasure separately . . . Well, it's tempting, just to look—now where are those Regents?

What would they be like, anyway, the best damn apples ever known to humankind, or at least to the one with white whiskers?

"Oh, My Lord, what a morning." And, "Oh, Eve and Adam." Of course you picked the apple long ago.

Eden, the Garden, is our culture's symbol for sacred pleasure. I am speaking here not of sacred pleasure's younger brother, *contentment.* Or its younger sister, *satisfaction.* Or even its distant cousin, *hedonism.* I'm talking about something deeper, about soul-singing, soul-touching rightness with the cosmos, joy so vibrant you can't just keep it all in your head because it makes your toes tingle, makes you want to break out dancing.

And it comes not from connection to what is easy or tasty or simply lovely to look at. It comes from something deeper—deep connection to that which is beautiful, or beloved. And that's why credit cards can't buy it, and McDonald's can't fry it, and jumbo jets can't fly it. It's too simple for that, too deep and slow, too primal. Too good.

Sacred pleasure comes from connection, significant connection, body and soul, to that which is beautiful—to autumn, or fugue, and reredos—or to what is beloved—partner, friend, child, or parent. Sacred pleasure.

"Oh Lord, what a morning!"

There are two Edens in the passages I read today. In the first, those who reach for sacred pleasure—the apple, arguably the source of life, of wisdom—are chastised by a judging God, told they will forever deal in sorrow and sweat to gain their bread. In these verses, Eve and Adam are chastised by a fate in which death, for them and their progeny, will always be stronger than love.

But in the other verses, something altogether different is portrayed, a birthing scene right there under the apple bough, generation upon generation, in the garden. And a bold declaration about the sacredness of passionate love, inextinguishable, unquenchable.

The two Edens depict different roles for humankind in relation to sacred pleasure. The one says, "No, never." The other, "Yes, always." The first says, "No you are flawed." The second, "Yes, you are blessed."

The scholars tell us that both of these passages appear to have had a long oral tradition preceding their emergence in written form. They both first appeared in writing at about the same time, ten centuries before the Common Era. The one from Genesis, which appears first in the Bible and sets up as the mythic archetype for the whole canon, was—must have been—chosen for that function. Someone, sometime, gave that particular story its powerful position.

I wonder why. A lot of people wonder why. There have been books written about it.

Given the choice that seems to have been there, why was original sin chosen over original blessing? Out of what kind of cultural loam did that emphasis grow and thrive so well? Why did we, at some early point of formation in our faith culture, home in on our own depravity more than on our divinity?

It drove a wedge, that choice, put a paradigm in writing, made it in some sense less malleable, more rigidified. It drove a wedge between the word *sacred* and the word *pleasure*, which has never been fully removed.

And that wedged reality—the idea that we are born to suffer because of a deep and hopelessly flawed nature—pervades our culture still, way past the walls of its religious institutions, now. What is pleasurable is more likely sinful than sacred. And what is sacred is probably not too pleasurable.

That is why I experience this church and this faith tradition, with its emphasis upon the divinity of each human, as quietly revolutionary. Somehow, in our own communal loam, lies the intention to reseed Eden.

But go to any bookstore, and see the broader cultural reality. Where is the stuff of sacred pleasure there? Its most concrete manifestation, the erotic literature, has become defaced, turned into pornography. It is shelved in a back room, in a brown-paper wrapping, or has been moved to a seedy little operation on some other street. Shame.

And what about the self-help section, the biggest in the store? Isn't that about sacred pleasure—finding out how to be happy and whole? Yes and no. Look at the titles. The overwhelming majority deal with fixing some flaw deep within ourselves, or within those around us—our codependency, our addiction, our post-traumatic stress syndrome, our depression, our mania, our brokenness, our brokenness, our brokenness.

It is good those books are available because that brokenness, those struggles, are real. But their sheer volume does tell a cultural story, does suggest that we remain within a paradigm that implies that somehow, deep inside, we must always—eternally—struggle with our flaws.

Get your hand away from that apple. A little pleasure, that's one thing, but don't take too much. No. The best you can expect is to pull yourself up from more flawed to less flawed. That's about normal, and if you ever get there, well, good. Okay. But don't hold your breath.

Some years ago, a therapist asked, "But what do you want?"

"All I want is for this anxiety to end. All I want is a little peace of mind at the end of a day," I answered. I couldn't imagine past that, couldn't think past the absence of pain and into the presence of deep joy. Never occurred to me.

It's not all that easy, for many of us, to find the road that veers mystically east and south on the far side of the Mendota Bridge. Yet even in our seeming cultural disdain for sacred pleasure, even in our deep doubt that we would ever belong in Eden again, there are signs—subtle and not so subtle—that we still cling to the idea of our own blessedness.

In *Sacred Pleasure: Sex, Myth and the Politics of the Body— New Paths of Power and Love,* cultural historian Riane Eisler has written:

Candles, music, flowers, wine—these we all know are the stuff of pleasure—the stuff of romance, or sex and of love. But candles, flowers, music and wine are also the stuff of religious ritual, of our most sacred rites.

Is it just accidental that passion is the word we use for both deeply pleasurable and also mystical religious experiences?

She makes a case that even though the first version of Eden, emphasizing original sin, has prevailed, we bear, deep in our cultural memory, the other version, which celebrates original blessing.

Riane Eisler is not the only one making this case. There are others from all strands of intellectual and cultural understanding, who are re-imagining, re-membering, and re-assembling, the second Eden, in which humanity is invited to know and experience a deep connectedness to what is beautiful, to what is beloved.

Our own Intentional Spiritual Community for Social Outreach* has found for us a most unusual version of that. The group has studied the work of two men from Northwestern University, outside Chicago, named John McKnight and Jody Kretzman. These two visited hundreds of urban communities across our nation, interviewed thousands of people, watched what people were doing to help make neighborhoods productive, vital places.

The results of their study were shocking. They found that the most successful efforts to revitalize neighborhoods had one thing in common. They all emphasized the giftedness, the divinity, of their residents, versus the brokenness. And with that in mind, McKnight and Kretzman devised a new, a different, strategy for neighborhood revitalization that is counter-cultural, exciting.

---

* Intentional Spiritual Communities at Unity Church combine action with the BeFriender ministry reflection model. See "Sources."

Instead of analyzing neighborhoods in terms of what is wrong — how much crime, how many shootings, how much poverty, drug-dealing, gang activity, rape—they invite people to begin instead with what is right—how many gifts the people there have, how many skills and talents, how many groups working together, how many resources.

Getting funding for this kind of neighborhood work is difficult, of course, because most foundations are conditioned to think in terms of human failure, in terms of what seems to be missing. But that has stopped neither McKnight and Kretzman nor the people catching on to the power of their idea.

If we would choose to explore the neighborhood around our church, choose to play a role in its vitalization with this paradigm, we would not step out looking for problems to fix, wounds to heal, or flaws to correct. We would step out looking for gifts to build upon and celebrate.

Maybe the man down the street is an alcoholic. That's one way to describe him. But what about the equally valid fact that he is a mechanical wizard, can fix anything that's broken, get any machine to work? Could he somehow be connected to folks who need his talents?

And that woman who's on welfare, the one with lots of kids. It's easy to see her in negative terms, as a drain on society. But how is it that everybody from her block gathers on her porch? What about her resilience, her courage, her determination to not give up that others find so inspiring they gravitate to it without even knowing why? And how might we use that gift she has for the betterment of the whole neighborhood?

McKnight and Kretzmann tell of a school that lost funding for its art teacher. Those in the neighborhood, understanding this paradigm, this belief in the goodness of people, did a gifts inventory of folks within a six-block radius. They found, in interviewing people, more than a hundred different artistic talents, from oil painting to mask-making to macramé. Of those hundred-some people, about sixty, as I recall, were willing to give time to teaching the schoolchildren what they knew. Sacred pleasure. Deep connections.

"Oh Lord, what a morning!"

Viktor Frankl's *Man's Search For Meaning* undoubtedly provides the most moving testimonial to the value of sacred pleasure. This sounds crazy, but he found a way to hold on to Eden, even in a Nazi concentration camp, even in Auschwitz. By his own explanation, that is how he survived—by refusing to let go of Eden. By holding in imagination, by holding relentlessly in memory, the apple of his eye—his beloved, his greatest, deepest source of pleasure, his wife:

> We stumbled on in the darkness . . . the guards driving us
> with the butts of their rifles . . . Hardly a word was spoken:
> the icy wind did not encourage talk. Hiding his mouth be-
> hind his upturned collar, the man next to me whispered sud-

denly, "If our wives could only see us now! I do hope they are better off in their camps . . ."

That brought thoughts of my own wife to mind. And as we stumbled on for miles, slipping on icy spots, supporting each other time and again, dragging one another up and onward, nothing was said, but we both knew: each of us was thinking of his wife . . .

My mind clung to my wife's image, imagining it with an uncanny acuteness. I heard her answering me, saw her smile, her frank and encouraging look. Real or not, her look was more luminous than the sun . . .

A thought transfixed me: for the first time in my life I saw the truth as it is set into song by so many poets, proclaimed as the final wisdom by so many thinkers . . . I understood how a man who has nothing left in this world may still know bliss, be it only for a moment, in the contemplation of his beloved . . .

I did not know whether my wife was alive, and I had no means of finding out; but at that moment, it ceased to matter. There was no need for me to know; nothing could touch the strength of my love, my thoughts, and the image of my beloved . . . "Set me like a seal upon thy heart, love is as strong as death."

The embrace of sacred pleasure need not be understood as an indulgence, a thing that you get to after all the problems have been solved. It is instead a way of being in the world.

The one who first sang those words, "My Lord, what a morning," the one who found a kind of ecstasy or rapture, a kind of sacred pleasure, in the falling of the stars as the light broke forth—that one was not singing from a point of comfort. That person was a slave, an American slave, choosing to rest the eyes of his or her soul upon Eden, the beauty of God's creation.

And for you, what is that?

What is beloved to you? beautiful beyond compare? Your passion, whether it smolders now or burns outright? Not the easy pleasure, the quick or obvious one, but the deeper, slower, simpler, more primal one—sacred and sometimes difficult to trust?

What is it, the Eden that not even an angry, judging God can steal from you if you claim it because it gradually comes to grow and live so deep inside you? The apple of your eye? What is it? And will you trust it?

—September 8, 1996

Turning it over

God stir the soil,
Run the poughshare deep,
Cut the furrows round and round,
Overturn the hard, dry ground,
Spare no strength or toil,
Even though I weep . . .
—*Earth Prayers from Around the World*

Human dignity resides in the capacity to participate in a
creative process, in short, in the capacity to be transformed.

What is presupposed here is that human beings live
in and through and from each other. We depend on
each other's sensitivities and feelings . . . the feeling of our
own situation with its possibilities, and also the feelings
of the other person's feelings. The creative process, then,
demands the continuing transformation of persons moving into significant novelty through creative interchange
. . . Transformation requires power, two kinds of power.
Both kinds of power are inherent in the process of becoming . . . The power to exercise an influence must
become effective, but something more than this active

power is required. The capacity to be influenced, a capacity to develop and respond to new sensitivities, is requisite . . .

In this sense we "create ourselves" as we go, to be sure always in relation to others.

—*James Luther Adams*

Turning it over. Time keeps turning it over, the unstirred soil of our assumptions. With her wild sickle of paradox, her flying plow of unpredictability, turning it over and over.

My great grandmother, Mary Barney, at the turn of the century, bought a plot of land along a lake and upon it built something she called a camp—a row of simple cabins, a dock, a sailboat, a canoe, an ice house, and a raft for the children to play on. She lived in the one on the far end, down by the bay where the sunrise played. The others she gifted to her children.

The one, the red one in the middle, became the communal eating place. The cook and his wife lived there, not the family. Sam Carlson, on the farm to the east, brought eggs and milk each morning. Esther Wannous, on the farm to the west, did the laundry.

She established a schedule, my great grandmother, one lovingly enforced with a large triangular gong, one that I—three generations later—can still recite, such was its clarity and power.

Her camp took hold of our clan. Children, and children's children, moved far away—to Boston, Toronto, the hills of northern California—yet still find their way to return each summer. I was first taken there at the age of six weeks, driven up from Chicago at my mother's breast. It is in my blood, this place. I know the very earth there. Its contours are my own.

It has changed, through all these years. The sickle of time has turned much over there. Each cabin has its own kitchen now; a cousin lives in the old dining hall. The gong has fallen silent. Sam Carlson and Esther Wannous have long since been replaced by a supermarket and laundromat in town. The ice house—torn down.

My grandparents' whole generation has died, now, and of their children, most have died, too.

Camp is presently occupied—or perhaps I should say governed—by four steely elders—my Aunt Sis, my Aunt Anne, my Aunt Jean, and the youngest of their era, my mother, Polly. We, their children, visit with our children, who run through the woods as we once did, barefoot and free, and even so, deeply aware of the now-silent gong. And it is an important place we return to.

But I want to tell you about the dock. Every year, as the season opens, someone has to put up the dock. For years it was the men, who—even into their seventies, their eighties—told the rest of us how to do it. And almost every summer, my Uncle Charles, who was an architect, and my father, Alexander, a dredging contractor, got into fiery debates on the topic. I remember, as a little child, wondering how long I would be able to hold up the edge of a dock section, how long my arms would last, while the two of them argued a point of engineering opaque to their helpers.

Last summer, though, with Uncle Charles, Uncle Mel, and Uncle Armas all buried in the earth and my father's knee giving him trouble, it looked to me like we needed a new plan. I had a husband of my own and two strapping sons. I was sure I knew the steps as well as I knew the shape of the earth curving along the shore.

So we went up early last year. I wanted to surprise the others. I thought they would be pleased to pull into camp, take that first lovely walk down to the lake to see how things looked, and catch sight of one task already handled.

It was harder than we thought. We got it crooked first, then got it straight. We laughed a lot, called out to our wise ancestors in the sky. "Now how did you to do that, Charles?" "Armas! Advice!"

In the end, it stood well, straight and sturdy as ever. We rested on it for a while, wrenches in our pockets, then drove back to the Twin Cities. This had been in some sense a rite of passage for my sons. Men, not boys, after all, put up the dock at camp.

I got a call from my mother, later, after they had all arrived at camp. "Thank you for putting up the dock," she said. But I, from our years together, could hear the hesitation in her voice.

"Was that all right?" I asked, suddenly unsure.

"Yes, of course. It was fine," she went on. "It's just that you put it in the wrong place."

"What do you mean? It's where we always have it, where the shore is sandiest, near the big rock."

"Yes, I know," she said. She was feeling embarrassed, I could tell. "But Sis and Anne and Jean all think it's not in the right place. It's too far over from the rock."

"You're kidding . . ." I whispered, wondering how I could have made such a mistake. "How much too far over?"

"Well, Sis says, about a full six inches . . ."

Ahhh . . . but I am the one in the pulpit. If Aunt Sis were here, the story would be told in quite another way. Perhaps more like this . . .

My niece Gretchen, she always has been the dreamy one. The one to plunge ahead, ignoring the details. I taught her how to sew, and her cross-stitch was as careless as they come. And Jeanny taught her about cooking and never could get her to measure anything, was always catching her pinching and guessing, as though a measuring spoon were her mortal enemy.

So now she's put the dock up, careless again. She probably thinks it's fine. But it isn't. It's in the wrong place.

I suspect her heart was in the right place. It usually is, but in truth, we did not need her help at all. I had it figured out. My nephew was coming later. He was willing to set it up, and then I would have been there—we all would have been there—to make sure it was the way we wanted it to be.

Because there is a lot she doesn't know, my dreamy, careless niece. She doesn't know that when I watch from my hammock on the hill over the lake, I can just see the grandchildren playing, or fishing, or building their castles in the sand there. And that this is one of the joys of my life. Where she put the dock, all I can see from that hammock is a clump of birch trees.

And she probably doesn't know—doesn't remember—that her Aunt Annie has been losing her sight these past years, that she has memorized where the trees are and the roots in the path, the juts in the road, the stairs to the lake. And she has memorized where the dock is so that she can find it without sight. Six inches off disorients her; not that she couldn't adjust, but she wants it there, where it has always been, for years and years and years . . .

We didn't need her to go and do what she did.

Turning it over. Time keeps turning it over and over, the untilled soil of our assumptions, the rambling, spreading garden of the generations. Change, novelty, never ceasing. It cannot be held back, made to freeze. It never stops.

We have our ways of embracing the past, of remembering it— good ways.

We sing the beautiful, beautiful songs of our ancestors, call to the hills as they did, shaping our words in their ancient tongue, as a way of rooting ourselves deeply and well, as a way of understanding something about the trajectories of our own motion through time.

We return to camp with our children, to hear the silent gong. We enter the sanctuary that held our forbears, and sit in the same pews, and sing the same hymns—good ways.

But there are times that each of us has yearned for it all to cease, this change, this motion, this turbulent movement of time. And nobody is immune to that.

Enough, I've had enough. I liked it better before. Before the computer era, before the days of single-parent families. You know, when you knew your neighbor, and time seemed slower somehow. I liked it better before there was the phrase "paradigm shift." I liked it better when my hip joint didn't hurt so much, when the dock was right, and Aunt Anne could see, was not going blind. Whatever it is. Whatever it is.

But we don't have that power—to stop change. We can wish for it, but we don't have it. We have two other powers instead.

James Luther Adams said it. Two powers: first, the power to instigate, that is, to put up the dock in a new place; and second —just as important, perhaps more important—the power to respond, that is, to choose how to act in relation to the way the dock got put up in a new place.

Gretchen, Aunt Sis: two powers in the presence of an infinitely complex cosmos constantly changing. The power to instigate or act and the power to respond.

Our dignity—our very dignity—our deepest freedom—lies in our capacity to participate in both kinds of power. For that is the very stuff of transformation, of creative interchange.

And as we find ways to open our hearts to that, to use our two powers well, we can come to trust change more, trust that each response we offer is also a new instigation; and each instigation, each act, a response to something preceding it. Trust that there is deep creativity embedded in the tilling of time itself, that our role of active and responsive participation is wonderful and precious and full of possibility.

Doesn't that sound good? Shouldn't we just love change, then? So what is the problem?

I invite you, for a moment, to ponder a change you've been through recently, or one you're experiencing right now. A challenging change, let's say, one you are in some sense resisting, that you have mixed feelings about.

Perhaps you can see, as I usually can in such situations, all the ways you can be both creatively active and responsive as this change unfolds for you, as the soil of your assumptions becomes tilled. Perhaps you can see the power that you have and how best to use it. The understanding is there. The acceptance is there. Even the willingness is there.

So why doesn't everything feel fine? Why aren't you content, overjoyed? Why aren't you at peace? What is causing your resistance? your pain? Is something wrong with you? I mean, what do you want? What's the problem? C'mon, c'mon, let's get going here. Lighten up, get with the program! What do you mean, six inches off? What is the problem? What is it?

One of you taught me, this summer, what it is. One of you, when I went to you and asked you to help me understand more about change, taught me something significant. In doing so, you instigated a kind of transformation within my heart. You acted upon me, and I, to my credit, in openness, responded.

And now I get it, something new, something valuable to me, about change, and why it often doesn't feel good, no matter how well we think we have it down. My own version, of what you taught me, goes like this:

Every shift in our lives, every paradigm shift—every change— gives birth to many, many children, gives birth to new ideas un- dreamed of before, new innovations, ways of doing things, ways of seeing and understanding. It gives birth to fresh approaches, unexpected relationships, creative paths. It gives both unantici- pated problems and solutions.

Every change, in a small way, literally gives birth to the cre- ative energy of the cosmos, and is precious for that.

But the firstborn child of any change is always Loss. And if you neglect that firstborn child, all the others suffer. That simple fact is crucial. Every change begins with the loss of something, its disappearance, its folding back and out of view. And that is a good-bye, and it needs to be tended.

No, your hip won't ever be quite the same again. You can prepare for the surgery and get through it, and be brave in the face of pain, but then you'll have a new hip. The old one, of which you had no consciousness earlier because it worked so well for you, that old one is gone, can't be reclaimed.

And computers are here, and the grand, elegant typewriter will be disappearing like a dinosaur. And nobody needs to be held to a schedule with a big, triangular gong anymore, and the ones who might reinstigate that are long buried under the earth. Now beepers, cell phones, they're something else again.

These are real losses. Ignore that, pretend it isn't so, and all the other births to come—all the siblings to follow—will be affected.

What do I mean, when I say tend to the firstborn child, the one whose name is Loss? I don't mean pamper it, or shower attention upon it. I don't mean wrap yourself around your loss, fixate on it, as though it's the only child of transformation. Because it isn't. It really isn't. People do that, sometimes. I do. It doesn't help much, in the end.

I do mean acknowledge it for what it is. Give it its name. Greet it. Welcome it into the world of your transformation. Let it grow, at its own rate, until it's strong enough to take care of itself. Then turn it over. Let it go, that you might tend to what is coming next.

Aunt Sis and I could have gone forward in a lot of ways. It was a story about a dock. But it was also a story about big changes for both of us. We sat down together, struggling to name our respective firstborns. We sat down with our two powers—the power to act creatively and the power to respond creatively.

Her firstborn was named Loss of Control. How could it be, that after all these years she would not be able to put up her own dock? How could it be that her sister was going blind? What else in her life was she losing control of? In which other arenas would she have to turn to others eventually? She named it for me. I invited her to do so.

My firstborn was named Loss of Sis and all that she stood for. Aunt Sis and Aunt Anne, Aunt Jeannie, were like mothers to me, all of them. I remember defying Jean's measuring spoons. I remember thinking that my cross-stitch looked like chicken tracks, and secretly laughing. How could it be, that after all these years, I could finally see that they were going to die? that my generation would have to figure out how to put the dock up because there simply wouldn't be anyone else? I named it for her. She gave me the space.

Creative interchange. I had been the instigator. I had tried for the big change, taken a shot at preparing for what was to come. She had been the responder: "Six inches off, you young whippersnapper." And now the thing was in motion, and the way it used to be, gone forever. There would never be another time that she didn't know that I, however imperfectly, could get that dock up without her.

We both knew it. It signaled a loss, and the beginning of a new era. And then our other children began to be born. First came my idea that we hire someone else altogether. To heck with it. It's just a dock.

Then appeared her idea that I just wait for her to get there before I plunge in (echoes of the measuring-spoon lesson). And so on and so forth. And then, this more amusing one, hers:

"Gretchen, anyone who wants to put a dock up right should first learn how to take it down. This year, why don't you and your husband and your boys take the dock down? A good lesson in how to proceed. And also helpful to the rest of us.

"Wait until we all go. Then do it. Just watch what you're doing this time. Maybe then when the time comes for you to put it up, well, you'll be ready." I liked that. And that's exactly what we did, just this past Friday.

I had put it off. Labor Day passed, then the next weekend and the next. Something in me resisted. Friday, it was cold, even more of an initiation rite for my sons than the day we first put it up over a year gone by. They were angry at me for making them go into the cold autumn water, impatient. They had their own ideas—strong opinions—about how I should have done it.

And some day, those opinions will threaten to reign. And I will stand on the shoreline like an old strong queen, like my Aunt Sis, and speak my piece.

Turning it over

Time keeps turning it over, the unstirred soil of our lives. With her wild sickle of paradox, and her flying plow of unpredictability. Let us claim our power, sing the songs of our ancestors, name the children of our fate, and then, by God, carry on.

—September 22, 1996

Journeying out . . .
and back again

And it came to pass after these things, that God did tempt Abraham, and said unto him, Abraham: and he said, Behold, *here I am*. And he said, Take now thy son, thine only son Isaac, whom thou lovest, and get thee into the land of Moriah; and offer him there for a burnt offering upon one of the mountains which I will tell thee of. And Abraham rose up early in the morning, and saddled his ass, and took two of his young men with him, and Isaac his son, and clave the wood for the burnt offering, and rose up, and went unto the place of which God had told him.   —*Genesis, 22:1–3*

This sermon may not seem to have been created in response to recent happenings in Washington, events related to the intense probing of the president's personal life. But it has.

You know the rest of the Abraham and Isaac story. Abraham takes Isaac to Moriah, asking that his son carry both knife and wood to be used for his slaughter. He binds Isaac to an altar and is about to kill him when the voice of God comes to him again, telling him to stop. Abraham again obeys without question.

But Woody Allen, in *Without Feathers*, gives this version:

And Abraham awoke in the middle of the night and said to his only son Isaac, "I've had a dream where the voice of the Lord sayeth that I must sacrifice my only son, so put your pants on."

And Isaac trembled and said, "So—what did you say? I mean when He brought this whole thing up?"

"What am I going to say?" Abraham said. "I'm standing here at two A.M. in my underwear with the Creator of the Universe. Should I argue?"

"Well, did He say why He wants me sacrificed?" . . .

But Abraham said, "The faithful do not question. Now let's go because I have a heavy day tomorrow."

And Sarah, who heard Abraham's plan, grew vexed and said, "How doth thou know it was the Lord and not, say, thy friend who loveth practical jokes?" . . .

And Abraham answered, "Because I know it was the Lord. It was a deep resonant voice, well modulated, and nobody else I know can get a deep rumble in it like that . . . "

And so he took Isaac to a certain place and prepared to sacrifice him, but at the last minute the Lord stayed Abraham's hand and said, "How couldst thou doest such a thing? . . . I jokingly suggest that thou sacrifice Isaac, and thou immediately runs out to do it."

And Abraham fell to his knees. "See, I never know when you're kidding."

The Lord thundered, "No sense of humor. I can't believe it."

"But doth this not prove that I love Thee, that I was willing to donate my only son on Thy whim?"

And the Lord said, "It proves that some people will follow any order no matter how asinine, as long as it comes from a resonant, well-modulated voice."

Yes! These resonant and well-modulated voices! I find myself returning to the story of Abraham and Isaac—all versions—again and again. Heard prescriptively—as a prescription for how to we ought to behave in relation to our God—I find it almost frightening. But heard descriptively—as a description of human nature—I find it fascinating.

Each time I return to it, I learn something more about myself, am given the opportunity to ask especially who my real gods are, for better or worse—meaning the forces to whom I tend to surrender—and also to ask myself what I have sacrificed—or betrayed—in their name. This time around, the story gave me a chance to ponder journeys out and back again.

Surely Abraham's story is one of the strangest in scripture. At first glance, it may seem that he learned something from his journey. After all, he set out intending to sacrifice his son and returned with his son alive and well. This is huge. It literally allowed for the continuation of the Hebrew tribes, for Isaac had been born very late in Abraham and Sarah's life, and he was an only child. His death could have been the death of a whole religious tradition.

It may seem that the journey accomplished much and generated much in terms of future events. But in one way it was close to meaningless as a transformational event: Abraham set out obeying God completely, and he returned—still obeying God completely. In terms of his relationship to that which he heard whispering to him in a well-modulated voice, nothing had changed for him at all!

Recently I attended the installation of Frank Revis, the new minister of first Universalist Church in Minneapolis. There I had the opportunity to hear John Beuhrens, president of the Unitarian Universalist Association (UUA), tell this story, perhaps yet another version of the same thing:

The owner of the general store in a small prairie town was sitting on his porch swing, when a stranger rode up on a horse. He said, "I've left home, sir, and I'm looking for a new place to settle down. Could you tell me what the people in this town are like?"

The store owner replied, "Sure I'd be glad to tell you what we're like here. But first, tell me what the folks were like in the town you left behind."

"Oh, they were bad news," the journeyer said. "They cheated, they lied, they stole. They were grumpy, as a rule, and in general they were a bunch of no-good half-baked lazy bums."

"Hmmm, I see," said the store owner. "Interesting. Well, I'm afraid you'll find the people in this town a great deal like that. If I were you, I'd keep on riding."

A little while later, another stranger rode up on a horse. "I'm looking for a new place to settle down. Could you tell me a little something about the folks in this town?"

"Sure I can. But first, tell me about the people in the town you come from."

"Oh, they were good people. They made mistakes, sure, but their hearts were in the right place, and they were, in general, kind and loving, courteous, and downright respectful to one another."

"Funny you should say that," mused the store owner with a grin. "I think you'll find the people in this town a whole lot like that. I think you might want to stay put, right here with us."

The owner of the general store knew that both journeyers were carrying something with them—carrying assumptions with them that, no matter how many miles they rode, they likely would not leave behind.

There's a strange quality about all of our journeys out and back. There's a way in which, though we may leave much behind us as we set out, we also bring much with us. Kind of like turtles, we carry our own reality along, and in so doing, conceivably can miss vast expanses of new landscape. We may think we're exploring new external arenas when really we're only staring at the same old thing. My, that mountain in the distance looks just like the inside of my shell!

You set out on the journey obedient to this or that thing and come back obedient to it still. You set out knowing that people are bad and find on your journey only bad people. You set out to switch jobs because the boss is so difficult and return to—surprise—a new job with another difficult boss.

You leave a faith tradition because it seems too confining or imposing and find another that, gradually over the years, seems to grow more and more confining, more imposing. You set out with no sense of humor and can't even tell when God is joking.

Abraham wasn't the only one. "Here I am, Lord," he said no matter where he was—trekking out from home, standing on a mountain, or stretching out his son on some kindling. And yes, in all those different places, he remained in a strange way exactly where he already was—bent in blind obedience. And he was not the only one: neither the first nor the last. We all are capable of doing this, in our own ways.

I know that I am, and I recall all too well one story from my own past about blind obedience, unreflective action.

My church, at that time, was in the middle of Minneapolis, and I was a seminary student. Some of our members lived in a pretty rough neighborhood. It so happened that prostitution began to increase in that neighborhood, to the extent that sometimes a fellow congregant, or her daughter, waiting for a bus, was approached by a john, someone offering money for tricks.

Something in me was enraged about that, and I immediately grasped—because of my training in the Saul Alinsky* mode of operation—that something could be done.

---

* See "Sources" for his books on radical action in neighborhoods.

I did not ponder why that particular situation triggered my anger. I did not just get quiet and look inside myself for deeper clues. I did not pray or take deep breaths, did not speak with those wiser than I in the quiet behind a closed door.

Instead I acted. I mobilized. I incited. Before long, I had a group of about twenty angry congregants—actually, it was more like forty of fifty—who were willing to act with me. We called it "doing an action" back then. We were going to do an action to stop the injustice.

First, we had to pick a target. Nobody wanted to go after the prostitutes. We figured their lives were hard enough already. So we decided to go after the johns.

Then, conversing with the police, we learned that these johns typically drove in from the suburbs because they wanted to keep this part of their lives far from their homes, their families. They were not part of the neighborhood and didn't care about how they affected people there. We also learned that all the police stings to date had been aimed at prostitutes—officers posing as johns, arresting women.

We asked the police to reverse their procedures for this neighborhood and go after the johns for once. Why beat up on those already in economic straits, already victims in their own way? When the police said no, we were angry, even a bit self-righteous.

Someone said, "I know how to get the cops to do what we want. Call in the TV show *Current Affair.* They'll come cover it, and that'll put the pressure on." So I, the leader of all this, called *Current Affair*, never having seen it and having no clue, therefore, as to what kind of show it might be. Unreflective action is blindly obedient. And any god will do.

You might guess that *Current Affair* picked it up immediately. After all, the topic was sex. (I think we're seeing something similar in the media this week.)

The people there told me to gather my congregants for some press events and said that if I could find some women to stand on the corner to pose as prostitutes, we could create our own sting. They'd get it on hidden cameras, and it would appear on national TV. This would be so embarrassing for the police and the johns that the neighborhood surely would clean up immediately. They would be there in a week.

I was able to organize my congregants to lead a neighborhood candlelight vigil for cleaning up the neighborhood, which *Current Affair* got on tape. We had a public confrontation with the police, which they got on camera too. The local press was there as well—they also are drawn to coverage of sex-related topics, I learned.

But I couldn't find a woman—not a single woman—willing to pretend she was a prostitute, stand on the corner, and do a sting. It was too weird, too scary. So I told *Current Affair*—sorry, we can't do that part. But, they informed me, this part—this filming of the sting—was the only part they really wanted. It was the part that watchers of their show would be most interested in, they said, and I had promised I'd fix it for them, and if I didn't come through for them now, well, anything could happen . . .

It was a veiled but clear enough threat. I was scared, but I did not stop to contemplate what my fear meant or how I might best grapple with it. It was signaling something to me, but I was moving too fast to heed it.

Finally the cameraman said, "Lady, why don't you just do it yourself? It's no big deal." Easy for him to say.

So I watched a prostitute operate for about an hour. I watched how she signaled to the men, and how the conversation seemed to go. And then, I went out there and stood on the corner. And I was just, plain scared. My skin was crawling with fear.

Finally, a man pulled up and asked me to get in his car. My job was to keep him talking to me until they had a chance to get their juicy film coverage with their outstanding telephoto lenses, including a zoom on his face and on his license plate. Then, I was to go immediately into a shouting, enraged mode, telling him he was going to be on *Current Affair,* how I hoped his wife would see it, and "Now get out of this neighborhood and never, ever come back."

After I did that, when I returned to the place where the camera was hidden, I was shaking. My knees felt about to buckle.

"Now am I done?"

"No, we need a couple more."

And so we repeated this routine about three more times. And then they said they were done, and I stopped. There was a terrible pain inside of me, but I did not stop to dwell on it.

Current Affair left town, and sure enough, there we all were on TV the next week. Our action did force the police to try to save face, and they began to train some of the women officers in Minneapolis to do stings on johns.

Our action definitely scared johns away. I don't believe my congregant's daughter was approached for one single trick on her way to the school bus, from the moment of that show's release until the end of the school year. But by the start of school the following fall, that neighborhood was exactly—exactly—the way it had been before.

This had been, in a very real way, a journey out and back again—one that led to nowhere.

The significant journeying in this case began for me only years later as I gave myself permission to contemplate what had happened, what I had done, and where I had traveled. I began to try to understand somehow, to look deep inside and develop an internal life more relative to my external one.

I got comments, at first, especially from those who saw the shift, which was not very subtle: "Hey, I thought you were big on social action. What, have you lost your zip these days? Gone into navel-gazing?" I knew that such comments meant nothing compared to the utter desolation of an unexamined journey. And for a not-so-gentle reminder, I had a strange videotape—of myself posing as a prostitute on *Current Affair*. And I still don't want to just go out obedient and then come back obedient again. And I still don't want to go to a new town and find the people there the same as the ones I left behind.

Still, I want to journey. I want to journey really and in a meaningful way. And that means, paradoxically, that I must regularly not journey.

I must be completely still, allow myself a posture that could easily be construed as immobility or indifference, something that looks indeed like "just sitting there," that *is* just sitting there.

For I believe that most lives that grow magnificent in terms of exterior journey or accomplishment include the hidden discipline of just sitting there. Martin Luther King engaged in daily, lengthy prayer. Mahatma Gandhi spent an easy third of his waking hours in either walking or sitting meditation. By the end of World War II, I understand, Winston Churchill had guided all of Great Britain in utilizing what he later named his "secret weapon" against Nazi Germany—five minutes, just five minutes, of deep, silent reflection across the entire country, every evening at nine o'clock.

Action and reflection—reaching out and reaching in—the journey and contemplation of the journey—these are not polar opposites. They are instead traveling companions of critical importance to one another.

And either—without the other—leaves us exactly where we started: in blind obedience to we-know-not-what.

People tell me sometimes that those who just sit there are doing it the easy way—and that action, the momentum of the journey itself—is what really counts. I confess that the opposite is true for me. It is much harder for me to focus my spirit and soul for even five minutes than to act out of carelessly focused impulse for days and days.

In action, I can pretend I am doing something whether I am or not. I can lose myself in the easy flow of the movement. In intentional contemplation, there is no distraction. There is no place to hide from what I value, what I hope for, what I fear, or who I really am.

If Woody Allen can rewrite it, so can I:

And God said to Abraham, Journey forth now. Take that which you love—that which you love most of all—and give it up; offer it as a burnt offering on one of the mountains that I shall show you.

Abraham rose early in the morning and saddled his donkey and set out and went to a place far away, but not to the place he had been shown, and fell into deep contemplation of what he had been asked to do.

And Abraham—also known as Bill Clinton, or as Monica Lewinsky, or as William Ginsburg, or as Vernon Jordan, or as the White House Advisory something-or-other, or as NBC, ABC,

CBS, or CNN—also known as Everyman or Everywoman— Abraham remained there for a great length of time and would journey no farther, until the deep integrity of his divine inner voice had spoken.

—January 25, 1998

Embracing Prometheus

Henceforth we will not part. There is a cave,
All overgrown with trailing odorous plants
Which curtain out the day with leaves and flowers,
And paved with veined emerald; and a fountain
Leaps in the midst with an awakening sound.
From its curved roof the mountain's frozen tears,
Like snow, or silver, or long diamond spires,
Hang downward . . .
And there is heard the evermoving air
Whispering without from tree to tree, and birds,
And bees; and all around are mossy seats
Where we will sit and talk of time and change . . .
—Percy Bysshe Shelley

The stories are old, fragmented, left to us only on the shards of shattered pots, the aged crumbling pages of poets remembered or unremembered. The stories, the versions, are too ancient to be clear.

In some, it is told that Nyx, the giant-winged bird of the night, laid a humming, iridescent golden egg in the midst of the lightless mists of chaos, then brooded over it and brooded over it—for eons—until it cracked wide. From it then emerged Eros, Passionate Love, holding a torch, a flame—the first fire.

The shell of Eros, cracked in two, became Uranus, the sky, and Gaia, the earth. And blessed by the power of Eros, these came together in love and created many children—Uranus the father, Gaia the mother—all gods, immortal and mighty, filled with the powers of both earth and sky.

These gods, these children, called the Titans, titanic in their power, possessed, some of them, hundreds of arms or only one eye. Others breathed fire or were volcanoes or whirlwinds.

Gaia found them beautiful. Uranus, half-frightened by them, half-sickened by their strangeness, wanted to cram them into the deep folds of the earth. One of the children, Cronus, for this reason grew determined to deal a killing blow to his father, so that he could prevent his own entrapment and reign powerful over all of the Universe.

So the stories go, but no two tellings are the same. They are too ancient, too fragmented to be clear. Uranus, it is said by some, could not withstand his son's deathblow but spoke these final words: "Evil will beget only evil, my child. Yes, I will die at your hand, but be prepared, then, for one of your own children to murder you. Evil begets evil, from generation to generation."

And so did Cronus, when he became a father, greatly fear his own offspring. And he did consume them, one by one, the first five born of the union between himself and the goddess Rhea. He swallowed them whole at birth: first Hestia, then Demeter, Hera, Hades, and Poseidon.

Rhea, enraged by time he had done all that, devised a plan. When the sixth child, Zeus, was born, she wrapped a smooth and heavy stone in swaddling clothes and held it to her breast. Cronus came to her, took the rock and swallowed it whole, thinking it to be his own newborn child.

Rhea raised the sixth child, Zeus, in secret then, and watched him grow to adulthood, trained him to be a fierce warrior and a cup-bearer. And when the time came, she told him to carry to Cronus a secret, poisonous drink that would cause him to vomit forth all the other five children alive.

Zeus did as he was told, carried to his father the drink. Cronus gulped it down, unknowing, and then spewed out the others. When this happened, the great war of the gods was on. For Zeus, driven by fear of his own father, with all of his newly released brothers and sisters set out to conquer and destroy Cronus and all his Titan warriors, set out to conquer Olympus itself.

One of Cronus's warriors, though, one Titan, chose to cross over the battle lines, chose to align himself with Zeus and the other children against his own clan loyalties perhaps, because something in him saw the deep unnaturalness of Cronus's father-hood, that he would choose—that he could choose—to do harm to his own offspring.

This one, perhaps, remembered dimly the original fires of Eros, who remembered the bright and powerful and restless fires of love. This one's name was Prometheus.

So when Zeus and his brothers and sisters finally became victorious, became the new rulers of Olympus, Prometheus the Titan stood near, anticipating—at long last after so much bloodshed and war—peace among the gods, peace among the generations.

But he soon learned that it was not to be. For Zeus was too much like the very father he had overthrown—fearful of revenge, violent, unpredictable, dangerous, and distant.

Evil begetting evil, fear begetting fear, again.

Prometheus learned this well, when he spoke to Zeus of fire. For he had looked down upon the earth below Olympus, where mortals lived, and seen with an increasingly compassionate heart that they were cold and hungry. He had seen that while they did have some gifts from the gods, they lacked the most important one of all, lacked the one that would give them the greatest power to create, to thrive, to heal, to empower the forthcoming of whole new worlds.

Prometheus saw that the mortals lacked fire. And he saw as well that Zeus had intentionally withheld it from them, fearful of what they might become, fearful that humans possessing fire would be as powerful as the gods themselves. Repeatedly Prometheus begged Zeus to give the mortals fire, for he saw that they suffered. And always, over and over again, the god of the heavens, the god of the gods, refused.

The stories are so many, borne to us fragmented, on crumbled sheaves of pottery and poetry. It is not clear. It is never clear. It is never just one way, one story, but always complex, mysterious—versions and versions.

Some say that Prometheus, driven by a deep and now unceasing compassion for mortals, made his way by stealth to the fire at the core of the very chariot wheel of Zeus, which was the sun itself; that he took an ember and concealed it in the hollow of a giant fennel stalk, which he waved in the air to keep it alive, then journeyed with it as though in flight to where the mortals stood chill among the flameless rocks.

Some say that Prometheus then passed fire to the mortals, and remained with them, helping them learn how to use it, showing them all of its secrets, all of its dangers and powers and capacities, and thereby initiating them in the very powers that Zeus had expressly forbidden them to have.

Prometheus, whose compassion knew no bounds, who alone among the powers of Olympus saw that fire, like love, can be passed to another without loss because of its capacity to spread and grow, to be unlimited. He saw that this capacity was its greatest strength and also its greatest danger.

When Zeus learned of Prometheus's bold act, he was filled to bursting with rage. He devised a terrible punishment. Chaining

Prometheus to a craggy rock jutting out over the stormiest ocean in the coldest part of the universe, he sent vultures to eat his entrails every day. Because Prometheus was a god, he could not die, and he was therefore destined to suffer the pain of this eternally. For every night, in the bitter cold, his mangled body would reheal itself, only to be torn open again the following morning.

Some versions say that he remained—was not released—for thirty thousand years. Some say that in that time, tied to the rock at the ocean edge, he learned to love all that was around him—Earth, Ocean, stars, moon, mortality itself.

Some versions say that had Prometheus been willing to beg the forgiveness of Zeus or to withdraw fire from mortals—had Prometheus been willing to tell Zeus some of his secret knowledge—he would have been released.

But he was not willing. For him—and no story says why—the distinction between immortal and mortal, between god and human, had become less important than the sheer, unceasing power of love that filled him like a fire, like embers in a fennel stalk. And he chose to remain chained and endure.

So, by the time Prometheus was released, his depth of compassion had been tested and honed into something boundless. And his wisdom, his understanding of both mortality and immortality, had been refined in a furnace of endurance, into something pure and resounding.

No fury at Zeus, no impulse for revenge or craving for conquest, no sense of superiority over humankind or nature, remained within his scarred heart. It held only a strong, vibrant, liberating tenderness, a desire to sit and speak of time and change, to search for looks and words of love each lovelier than the last.

To my father, on Father's Day 1997:

Sometimes other people seem to have simpler ties. My ties to you have never been simple. You have always been such a powerful person in my life. And not at all unlike a god. I don't know why this has been so.

When I was small and you were gone, which was so often, gone down the big river on the big boats that I would only hear about but not travel on (for a little girl would not be allowed to travel on those wild things)—when you were gone, I dreamed again and again of where you were, imagined you as king, powerful ruler of the tide, the crew, the barge, the bridge. I imagined you to be the creator, the shaper of what lay beyond my own sight.

Had you been gentler—had you been a gentle man—perhaps your very presence, upon your return, would have cracked the iridescent egg of your godliness for me. But you were not gentle, not a gentle man. Instead, you were tempestuous—wonderful and terrible at once, unpredictable to me. To be afraid of you was easy enough. To be alongside you—especially to be with you on the river—was to be in Olympus itself.

I still remember, cannot forget, the roaring curve of the boat when you finally did choose to let me come with you, the spray of the water, and the sense of being about to capsize but not capsizing, learning in your presence that you knew how to wield this awesome power of yours, so that the river would not snatch me under.

I learned so early and so hard, somehow, to both love and fear your power—your creative forcefulness—in the world. I tell you—unceasingly, it awed me. Unceasingly. So that you were, to me—some kind of god.

And I, always, tried to understand your nature, your mystery, as though I could not, as though I were too small, too weak, without my own fire.

Today, I tell you that I see and celebrate, in you and in me, all the gods at once, just as from the mythical unfolding of these ancient stories come mysterious primal forces all simultaneously real, simultaneously important.

Today I see in you, in me, in all of us, the power of Nyx the great winged bird, to create order out of chaos; the power of Eros, original bearer of the fires of love; the power of Uranus, clear and starry strength of the sky; of Gaia, greening marble-veined force of the Earth; of Cronus, the capacity of evil to beget evil; of Zeus, the capacity of sheer uprising strength.

These are Titanic forces, Olympian forces, mysterious, looming and unfolding about us, and within us. But there is also the power of Prometheus—not to withhold but to pass on, pass on the hot fire of love, to blur the distinction between immortality and mortality, to blur the meanings of life and death, to have deep and unwavering compassion, to endure.

On this day, this Father's Day, I honor above all else, the Prometheus in you—you who, before I was born, from what you carried burning in your own loins, kindled the tinder in the lightless hearth that was my mother's womb and gave me the very fire of life itself, so that I became literally ignited then, in the utter and cavernous darkness there.

I honor you who gave me fire, that I might forge my way in this almost overwhelming world, who gave me your best wisdom, your best compassion; who, for my sake, has endured. I honor the Prometheus in you and acknowledge that I have received your fire, that it burns like a conflagration in my chest cavity, that it moves me, transforms me, ungentles me, that it bursts me out, sometimes hot and careless.

I acknowledge to you that I have received your fire, that it is my inheritance, and that it frightens me, this fire, this power, these gods in me and you and all of us. It frightens me like love and danger frighten me, like Nyx, Uranus, Gaia, Cronus, Zeus, Rhea, and mortality all frighten me. All that I have feared or loved in you lives on in me. The fear has been passed. The power has been passed. The love has been passed. The whole myth, fragmented, shattered but still intact, it has been passed. The fire has been passed.

Today I honor that you have given and I have received. And for this day, I name you, of all the names, Prometheus.

To my child, on Father's Day 1997:

Yes, I have been enduring, waiting for you to see, waiting for you to know, that the distinctions between gods and mortals are blurred, that we are one another's immortality, that the fire is in you as well, and all the rest. Let the time of my enduring be over. Let me say to you now only these, echoing Shelley's words:

I know of a cave somewhere
All overgrown with trailing plants
Which curtain out the day with leaves and flowers . . .
A fountain leaping in its midst makes an awakening sound
And there is heard the evermoving air
Whispering from tree to tree,
And birds and bees, and all are mossy seats . . .
There let us sit, you and I, and speak of time and change . . .
There let us search, with words and looks of love
For hidden thoughts each lovelier than the last . . .
Until our spirits, like lutes touched by the wind
Weave harmonies where dischord cannot be.
Then, believe me child, I have learned it all too well,
Then, and only then, veil by veil, shall evil and error fall.

—June 15, 1997

Grief and praise

You traveled all too briefly
through our varied worlds,
harvester of light.
You saw
an unseen light
and gave it to the world.

That light
you saw with special eyes
and would not be content
until it was gathered in and
shared with all of us
whose eyes are blinder than your own.

And now the light of distant places
and of things as yet unseen
have called you
beyond the edges of the known,
and there you remain,
harvester of light.

Yet in our hearts
go ever with the light.
Husband, son, brother, uncle, steadfast friend,
go ever with the light.
                                        —*John Shippee*

Up on the hilltop cemetery above the farm. Every year on this day our whole family meets to tend the tall white pillar. We clip the grass, plant a few geraniums . . . The nieces and nephews play leapfrog on the shorter tombstones. The mothers get after them, and the fathers say, "Oh, let them be."

An hour before at the lunch table, Dad and I had gotten into a "discussion" about the Holy Spirit. Was it a real spirit, like the wind (which is my opinion); or was it more like a person (Dad's, plainly explained to me with several helpful Biblical references.) It started out fine but got louder until we had to go to neutral corners. He thinks I'll burn in hell. I think he's crazy.

But now it's time to go. Only Mother, he, and I are left. We stand near our cars—they will drive about a mile to the farm, and I, five hours to Minnesota . . .

"Corn looks good, doesn't it?" Dad says.

I say, "I thought it was supposed to be knee high by the Fourth of July. It's already almost that."

He laughs a little and looks proudly down the hill. Then he drapes his arm across my shoulder. He chats for a minute about this and that, corn mostly, and I don't know whether I want him to take his arm away right now or leave it resting warm across my shoulder forever. He kisses my neck, once, very quickly, and with a casual wave gets into the car, not looking back.
                                        —*Brian Newhouse*

I have been learning more about grieving than I've wanted to, lately. And sometimes when you're learning more about something than you want to, it helps to turn to others. And sometimes, it helps if those others come from some other end of the earth. Because then their wisdoms spring out at you from a culture and a place you can't deny easily, because you don't really know much about that place in the first place.

I have been turning to, listening to, learning from the words of Martín Prechtel. One of you—Marie Burgeson—first told me about him.

I don't understand quite who he is, really. I know he grew up on an Indian reservation, that his mother was Pueblo and his father some mix of Austrian or Irish. I know that, sometime in adolescence, he wandered to Guatemala, where he finally found what felt like home in a little village among the Tzutujil Mayan peoples. There he found a mentor in one of its last remaining shamanic leaders.

I understand that in 1991, after eighteen hundred people there had been killed—many of them babies he had welcomed into the world himself—Martín Prechtel's hair turned white, and his body became knotted with pain. In finding his way through, he began to speak about grieving and praising in ways that others found wise.

Among the Tzutujil Mayan, there is no differentiation made between grief and praise. There are not even two different words for the concepts. They are the same word. This fascinates me.

In our culture, grief and praise are usually understood as separate, if not polarized. Praise tends to be communal and joyous; grief is more often private, tear-filled, and heart-draining. Praise takes you up, is something you come down from. And grief takes you down, is something you come up from. In what kind of place would grief and praise be understood as the exact, same place?

I have been learning from Martín Prechtel. At the core of the answer is this: Among the Tzutujil, life itself is construed as a monumental gift, a gift from the gods—not one but many— many spirits, all the holy spirits of the dead and the invisible, the wind spirits, people spirits, corn spirits.

These gods, these spirits, must be fed by the living, or they themselves will grow thin and gaunt, will die. And what do they eat, these spirits? What do they drink? What do they feast upon?

They feast upon human gratitude for life. Every mortal expression of love for life is to them as sweet as honey. And they are always hungry and always thirsty; they don't like to be gaunt and thin like Barbie dolls; they like to be fat. Big in the belly, big in the cheek. The task of mortals, then, is to feed them—to feed them with open and unreserved and constant expressions of love for life.

Grieving, among the Tzutujil, is literally food for the gods because it is expression of deep love for any life that has been lost.

And likewise, praise is food for the gods because it too is the expression of deep love for life, life that has not yet been lost, though surely it will be someday.

Grief or praise that remains unexpressed hurts the gods, starves them. And when they are starved, they cannot do their own work, which is to give life back to mortals in the many forms of babies and seeds, corn crops and trees, fresh water, rain and sun—all that is outrageously beautiful and life-giving. The relationship is symbiotic; it is an ecosystem of mortals and spirits, who must care for one another so that both—and all—may survive.

Open expression of grief and praise, among Tzutujil, then— sorrow and joy, weeping and laughing, groaning in pain or spinning in ecstasy—all of these are essentially the same thing. And all are expressions of love for the fleeting preciousness of life itself, and food for the gods.

The Tzutujil have two kinds of guides in this regard. The first are clerics: hierarchical religious leaders who conduct communal ritual. The second are shamans, not understood as holy people so much as people who love the holy, shamans who know how to bring others in touch with the spirits.

The word for shaman in the Tzutujil language can also mean singer, weeper, doctor, or spirit lawyer—one who knows about grief and praise, who negotiates for the well-being of the village, for the well-being of the spirit world, and for life itself.

The cleric might lead you in liturgy, as I am leading this morning. But the shaman will come to your home. And if you have lost something beloved and cannot weep, he or she will gather people around you and speak words intended to break through your inexpression, then also begin to weep, showing you what to do, until everybody around you is weeping, until grief is completely spent and turns then on a heartbeat into praise—a deep, strong, heartful expression of love for the life of that which is departed.

And if you still sit there like a stone, after all that, the shaman will take you to the ocean and dunk you in the healing water for hours—maybe for many days and nights—so that you sink to your neck in cold saltwater until your grief turns from a solid to a liquid, until you find your tears, and tear your clothes, and pull your hair out, and laugh and shout, in gratitude for what you have been given and then lost again.

This is not cruelty. This is doctoring, this is spirit-lawyering, done to save your life and to feed the gods, that they might in turn feed you, until you die in your time, and others gather to grieve for you, praising all that your life has meant to them.

Among the Tzutujil, grief/praise is so holy, so potent, that anyone who sees anyone else expressing it, knows to stop all activity and listen. Even if you hate that someone, even if she is your worst enemy, even if he weeps or becomes ecstatic in the street, you stop and listen.

In this way, nobody grieves alone. Nobody expresses love for life alone, no matter how long or painful or crazy or joyous it gets. This is a given, and there are rules of thumb. The recommendation is for at least fifty people around you, if possible. But a hundred is better. A thousand is better yet.

Martín Prechtel wonders whether Americans have grown violent—stony—because we have lost, in our radical individualism, basic wisdoms about grief and praise, because we try too much, too hard, to endure in isolation the monumental comings and goings of the gift of life. He argues with me—even in this case, of my going from this place, an event small in the grand scheme of things—he argues with me. He implies some way unlike the polite good-bye, the quietly closed door.

"Listen to the Eclectics!" he seems to say as they play here today.* "Let them be your shaman. Let their songs help you to feel what you are leaving. Let them help you to feel how beautiful it is. Let them help you weep for, and praise, help you leave this village you wander from." And I know how much the music touches me, thaws me out, dissolves the stoniness, and how much, because of that, it scares me.

Love for life, says Martín Prechtel—in either its grief form or its praise form, doesn't matter. Love for life must be both

---

* The Eclectics, a rock-and-roll band made up of members of Unity Church, occasionally play for Sunday services.

sung out, and listened to, not dwelt upon with a whining, self-centered morbidity, but shared. Else the gods, the holy spirits, grow thin and gaunt and choke life off at its source.

"Give praise—and receive it—abundantly, until you are spent," goes his advice. Not the manipulative kind, not the kind designed to get the other person to do what you want. But the real kind, where words of sheer gratitude fly out of your mouth like beautiful bright birds and also fly at you from others, as though you are a tree they have chosen to land in, flying right down your shirt and into the branches of your heart. Words, like beautiful bright birds that you almost want to shoot with sharp arrows of embarrassment or self-doubt or distrust. "But don't," he says.

Have you ever been to lunch with Bill Manning? From this quiet man among us, who has been so much my spiritual teacher, whenever we have lunch together, the bright birds fly in every direction. The person who seats us at the table, the waiter, the busser—all receive his praises, his gratitude. The soup, the bread, the sun in the trees outside the restaurant—he speaks of them all as holy, gifts of life to be celebrated, to be praised.

Bill knows how to do this and teaches me, as so many of you have taught me, and still teach me. Martín Prechtel is not the only one. It's not just about praise of what you've got but also about praise of what you've lost. Does that, too, really have to be both given and received?

This is beyond difficult for most of us; it's close to counter-cultural. It goes against almost everything we've been taught about independence and privacy and stiff upper lips and boot-straps. But it can be understood as yet another way to praise the outrageous beauty of life—either flying from you like a flock of beautiful dark birds or coming to you from others, and landing in the branches of your heart like a magnificent shadow with beating wings.

Have you seen the book from which I read the poem today—the one that posthumously honors David Shippee by sharing his photography? I love that book. Every page—every image—flies into the tree of my heart like a beautiful dark bird, and makes me glad for life, even life lost.

If David's family had succumbed to the private or the morbid, I—we—would have been deprived of the outrageous beauty of his artistry that is his life. They were wise enough not to do that. They—and many others among you—teach me about this hon-oring of life, which could be called grieving *or* praise. And you teach me how to give it, and how to receive it, and how not to shoot it but to let it fly.

About how not to be morbid or self-pitying about it but to let it fly. About how to keep the Holy Spirit alive, whether it moves in the wind or the Biblical words, or a corn crop, or a song the Eclectics sing, or a waitress who brings us bread and soup, or a harvester of light who has passed this way and gone. How to keep the Holy Spirit alive, how to keep the Gods fat, so that they can bring us life again, in all of its outrageous beauty.

Not amen this time, but—even through my fears—thank you, and all praises to you.

—October 18, 1998

Floaters

"I'll get right to the point, Winthrop," my grandmother said officiously. "I'll be dying some time after my sixtieth birthday and I don't want to be a burden on my family. I'm going to pick out the cheapest coffin you carry in this boneyard and I don't want no high-pressure salesmanship trying to get me to buy some million-dollar box."

Mr. Ogletree looked both hurt and offended but answered in a mollifying voice. "Oh, Tolitha, Tolitha, Tolitha, I am only here to serve your best interests . . . But Tolitha, I wasn't aware that you were ill. You look like you could live to be a thousand."

"I can't think of a more horrible fate," she answered.

—Pat Conroy

By my read, Grandma Tolitha had a pretty good point. We all die, and who would want to live to be a thousand anyway? We could stop right there, but the story goes on, with Mr. Ogletree eventually leaving Tolitha and her grandchildren upstairs to mull over the potential of an elegant mahogany casket offered at a slightly reduced price:

When we heard his footsteps on the stairway, my grandmother said, "It makes me sick to think that ghoul is going to see me buck naked when I'm dead."

"How disgusting, Tolitha," said Savannah. "We won't allow it. We won't even let him peek."

"He has to get you naked when he cuts open your veins to drain the blood. I guess it won't make that much difference to me then. I just wish it could be someone besides Winthrop Ogletree. You could add a little vinegar to his voice and pour it on a Caesar salad. Here, someone hold this."

She pulled a small Brownie camera out of her purse and handed it to Luke.

"What's this for, Tolitha?" Luke asked.

My grandmother moved a straight-backed chair over to the first casket Winthrop Ogletree had suggested. She carefully removed her shoes and climbed nimbly on top of it. We watched. I did not speak. She wiggled her toes and tried to stretch out. Then she closed her eyes and lay perfectly still.

"I don't like the way these box springs feel," she said at last, her eyes still tightly closed.

"It's not a mattress, Tolitha," Savannah said. "It's not supposed to feel like a hotel bed."

"How in the hell do you know how it's supposed to feel?" Tolitha asked. "Look, I'm paying quite a bit of money for this thing, and I'll be in it for quite a spell."

"Hurry up and get out of there, Tolitha," I begged, "before someone spots you and we all get in trouble."

"How do I look?" my grandmother asked, nonplused . . . "Take a few snapshots of me, Luke." . . .

Luke took a few pictures, shrugging his shoulders at us as he advanced the film and shot from different angles.

"Mrs. Blankenship's coming up the walk, Tolitha," I said in a half-scream. "Please get out of there."

"Who cares . . . "

Ruby Blankenship swept into the room, regal and inquisitive . . . "What are you Wingo children doing here?" she demanded. "Nothing has happened in your family for years."

Before we could answer, she spotted Tolitha lying peacefully with her hands folded across her stomach.

"It must've been sudden. I haven't heard a word about it," Mrs. Blankenship said . . . "Don't she look natural, kids? She almost looks alive."

"Yes, ma'am," Luke said.

"What did she die of?"

"I'm not rightly sure, ma'am," Luke answered, and there was real misery in his voice as he looked to us for assistance . . . Savannah walked to the window and looked out toward the river. Her shoulders were shaking and she was approaching hysteria. I was far too mortified to appreciate the hilariousness of the situation.

"What do you mean, you don't know?" Mrs. Blankenship demanded. "Was it her heart? Or some kind of cancer she picked up in Africa? I bet it was her liver. She was a very heavy drinker . . . "

As Mrs. Blankenship handed a stick of gum to Luke, my grandmother stopped her by reaching out and grabbing hold of her wrist. Tolitha, sitting erect out of the casket, then took the piece of gum, unwrapped it, put it in her mouth, and lay back down in the casket, slowly chewing the gum. There was a moment of absolute silence in that room before Ruby Blankenship screamed and bolted for the door.

Grandma Tolitha was privy to another wisdom as well, I think. Except for very special occasions—which you have to create for yourself in life—once your bones fall into that casket, they're there for a long time. So it stands to reason—a little practice can't hurt.

To get the overall effect, anyone might well choose to lie down really still, and squeeze the eyes shut, try, from within the light of life, to learn about complete darkness.

I figure that light and dark are both beautiful, in their way. That's what Ralph Waldo Emerson said, that it's all miraculous and only a matter of gradation. Day to night, night to day—neither begins at one marked moment.

When we dedicate new lives, as we do at Unity today, I'm always aware of how much bright light each baby radiates, how much potential, how much future movement and action and spending of outward energy each tiny baby is designed and prepared for and holds in its little hands and behind its dreamy eyes.

And when I do a memorial service at the end of someone's life—especially if it has been a long life—I'm always aware of how the initial exterior brightness of that life's beginnings have been expended into something graceful and full; how, in response to the gradual fading of the outer light of bodily life, the inner brightness has grown so that the soul exudes, even in physical death, a certain quality of warmth and completeness both invisible to the outer eyes and obvious to the inner eyes of loved ones.

The movement of birth to death is not unlike the words of that old hymn "Now Light Is Less"—daylight fades, moon skies grow wide and deep, wisdom moves, ripe then sere.

Some of you might know what floaters are, but most of you, I'm guessing, don't. I didn't until this past year. Floaters—at least the kind I'm talking about—come into your eyes.

I have been told we all have them. They are actually, I think, like debris on the surface of your eyes, those strange shapes that float into your field of vision like spots that almost seem like they're not there at all, that drift slowly, then translucently, beyond the horizons of perception.

For my husband, Tom, in this past year, floaters have become more severe. They're related to his diabetes, which he has had for almost thirty years now, since he was eighteen. His floaters got worse—went beyond translucency—when some blood vessels burst in his eyes and caused, not hazy, but large dark masses to come and go, blocking his vision more and more.

The treatment, eventually, was laser beams, thousands of laser beams around the periphery of each eye, to cauterize the blood vessels there and stop the bleeding. This diminished his peripheral and night vision a great deal, a necessary trade for saving some amount of his straight-ahead daytime sight.

For a long time we didn't even know whether the lasers would work. It took multiple treatments, months and months of pain in the eyes and diminishing vision, before his condition stabilized. Half the time I thought he was going to end up completely sightless, in a kind of dark that I found more frightening than beautiful. Everything in our lives was impacted—our parenting, our work, our home, our relationship.

Perhaps you have wondered, during these past months, why I stopped telling you stories about him, my motorcycle companion, my partner, my best friend. It was because I was confused by these floaters and all that they implied. There was no story I could tell without dipping into too much emotion.

Funny, I knew, in my head anyway, that they were nothing really, his floaters, compared to what some people experience in the way of transition or pain—disorientation. But somehow, knowing all that in my head just didn't help my heart very much. His floaters were big and opaque and blinding. I was afraid.

How would he handle losing his driver's license, if it came to that? How could he possibly cope with losing his ability to read, this man who averaged about a book a day? What would happen to his new business, which took every ounce of his sighted energy already? How he would be able to watch our boys out on the soccer or baseball field? And how would I ever figure out how to do what he couldn't do alongside what I was already doing?

I was also angry. Sometimes I'd forget—or ignore—that he could barely see, ask him what was taking him so long or why he seemed so distracted, so absent. There was a voice in me that said harshly, "Well, so what? You won't be the first person on this earth to go blind. Other people figure it out. Don't expect me to baby you or feel sorry for you."

I was also, perhaps most of all, overtaken by a strange and debilitating numbness. Once I was on my way to pick him up at the hospital after a laser treatment, and I drove straight through a stop sign. The policeman who pulled me over was kind.

"Lady, are you okay? Is there something you're worried about?" he asked, studying my face.

I could have said, "Yes, I'm worried about my husband's sight, and I'm on my way to pick him up at the hospital right now." But that didn't occur to me. I was numb, didn't know I was upset.

So I just mumbled, "No, I'm fine . . . fine. "

"Well, take care, and for God's sake pay attention now," he said gently, handing me the ticket.

Over the months, I thought about it and thought about it, inner light and about outer light. And I knew that what frightened me most about my husband's dark, massive floaters was that they signaled the dimming of his outer light. They reminded me that he is going to become frail of body, eventually, and then die. As am I.

Like Grandma Tolitha practicing death on her grandchildren and Mrs. Blankenship, our family too was getting a little practice with the fading of bodily strength, a little practice with the dimming of daytime, the movement of the light from body to soul.

Tolitha called it, much more gleefully, a trial run. I, for my part, just couldn't seem to laugh.

Tomorrow may look different, but today I see that each of life's transitions—each challenge, which so often begins with a ripping loss and ends with deep gain of wisdom—each transition is, in some sense, a practice for the biggest transition we will face in our lifetimes—the transition from life to death.

It is the shift to complete outer darkness, the body in a casket or an urn for a long, long time; the shift to inner light, the soul released into mystery and memory and spirit. Magnificent, terrible, wonderful transition—totally natural and totally terrifying.

And the one thing I learned, in my own little practice session, was that there is no need to do it—any of it—alone. Even Tolitha knew that, fearless as she seemed. It would not have been the same—it would not have even worked, in terms of her own soul's growing brightness—had she gone up those winding funeral parlor stairs alone, and lain down in that casket alone, and never spoken to anyone else about it. She needed people, needed other souls there. She needed people to laugh with, to play with, to take her photograph, and to snatch gum from.

I, too, eventually found that to try to get through a transition—big or little—alone, was unnecessary and perhaps even silly. The hands that helped me, those hands I will never forget. Neither will I forget the ears that listened or the eyes that looked upon me with inner light.

These eyes and ears and hands were nothing sensational in terms of professional expertise. They were just holy, holy, holy as the grubby fingers of Luke who held the camera and took the unthinkable snapshot, willing to be present, to witness.

Even throughout this frightening rehearsal for the biggest transition of all, others helped. My mother, bless her heart: "Are you having a hard time dear? What can I do?"

"Towels, I think I need towels." It was crazy talk. I didn't need towels. I was confused.

But my mother brought me towels and also soup and a shrimp salad that was nothing short of manna.

My father: "Are you coming out okay? These medical bills can be terrible." My father, convinced that he's hopelessly doomed to hell for sins the rest of us can only imagine, who doesn't even think of money as ministry.

My friends Anne and Kathy, who met me for coffee just every so often, who never once said, "You sound half-crazy." Just "Yes . . . uh-huh . . . tell it . . . tell it again . . . tell more."

My husband, too—half-blinded and so deeply discouraged, staring into a deep outer darkness—he was holy. "Well, I can't help you now, so you just do what you have to do. Just take care of yourself. "

You know, those of you considering service to the church as parish visitors—or *any* of you who may present for others in difficult time, in times of transition—you need to know that it is not about professional expertise. It's about being willing to witness other human beings practicing their transitions, practicing what it means to go through the mysterious cycles of loss and gain, gain and loss, dimming and brightening, living and dying.

The main question is never "How can I fix it?" Because it can't be fixed, this movement, this never-ending spinning, cycling. Neither can it be halted. Always, instead, the question is "How can I be present to you in your experience of it?" And the answers—the answers we give to one another out of the experience of a transition—are never predictable, and often, wholly mysterious.

"Towels? If you say you need towels, let's talk about towels then. I would have thought you needed a hug, or a trip to Hawaii, but hey, if you say towels, well towels it is."

"You want me to photograph you in that thing?"

"Well, I'm listening."

"You don't have any hope left at all? Completely trapped?"

"I'm listening."

"Floaters? What are they? Tell me."

If you think about it—how really complex and mysterious it all is, this transitioning, this cycling through life—you can eventually get to the point where Grandma Tolitha was, playing with it, making sure it warrants the taking of a photograph or two.

But some of us are more like Mrs. Blankenship. We scream in terror. Some of us look silently off alone, like Savannah gazing out the window of the funeral parlor. Some of us, like Luke, end up holding the camera.

We are—each and all of us—rare uniqueness needing company, through transitions little or big or gigantic—needing witness. Lights we all are, dimming on the outside to brim on the inside. Nights we are, unique wisdoms growing ripe, like skies becoming wide and deep.

Why would anybody want to do all that alone?

—October 4, 1997

Blessings

And he lifted up his eyes, and said,
Blessed be ye poor:
for yours is the kingdom of God.
Blessed are ye that hunger now:
for ye shall be filled.
Blessed are ye that weep now:
for ye shall laugh.
                              —Luke, 6:20–21

Have you ever had more things happening to you at once than you can possibly process or understand? when everything's just too fast and too frightening? The church burnings that have been hitting the news lately must be such times for the people directly experiencing them.

Those of you who have been at Unity Church for a while must remember the fire here, how disorienting, how intensely disturbing it was. Think of grappling with that kind of experience, adding to it a fear that the fire was set by someone who hates you sight unseen.

Questions, worries, fears, confusions—fast and frightening. Why is it happening? Why are we doing this to one another? Predominantly black churches thirty-five now, mostly white churches more than two dozen, southern churches and now some northern ones, have burned. Why? Why are we turning one another's holy ground to cinder?

There are times—sometimes long stretches—when life just seems to flow along at a peaceable rate, calm river. Things happen, people come and go, workdays wash past one another, children tug at your shirttails, there's an almost ho-hum evenness to it, a rhythmic smoothness.

And then suddenly, it becomes all turbulence—white water, whirlpool, riptide, undertow. Events begin to rush and tumble, pile in on you in overwhelming ways. Things happen faster than you can think them through. You feel washed away, swirled around, confused, frightened. It somehow turns all twisters and tornadoes just when you were expecting a little breeze, turns to big sweeping forest fires, bonfires, when you had only planned on lighting a candle.

A part of me dreads these times, these experiences of turbulence. Something else in me is deeply respectful, sometimes even appreciative, but usually not until they are long past, if ever.

What these times do bring in their aftermath, their wake, is invitation to spiritual deepening, increase of wisdom. The burning of churches this summer is one among many cultural opportunities to see greater spiritual depth. But there are plenty of personal opportunities too.

My good friend Roy is twice my age, a World War II veteran, a cement contractor, a man who's spent the bulk of his life in hard physical labor. His hands, gnarled with muscle and strong as thick leather, tell his story well. I like his hands. And all of him.

Son of a pious Catholic woman and her rakish one-time husband, Roy is both tough and tenderhearted. About five years ago, when his giant, strong body gave in to arthritis and would labor well for him no longer, he retired, bought a trailer in a small town up north, and immediately befriended the bulk of the children in the trailer court, especially those who ran loose and unsupervised while their parents worked.

All the children call him "Grandpa" now and accept his peanut-butter sandwiches and his clumsy leather-handed hugs, and they sing along when he plays his guitar. It's really a good thing—for him and them, I think—one of the most moving ministries I've witnessed.

Ever since I've been ordained, Roy has been asking me for one thing—to baptize him. I, for my part, have been refusing. The conversations go something like this . . .

"But Gretchen, my mother is worried about me going to Hell! Just baptize me. You know, sprinkle a little water on, say a few words, so she can relax."

"But Roy, I'm Unitarian-Universalist—and you're—what are you, anyway? Baptize you into what? I don't even know how. If you want to make your mom happy, why don't you go join the Catholic church?"

"Because I'm too sinful to be Catholic anymore. It's too late! Couldn't you just—you know—give me a little splash?"

This went on—the way things between friends can—for years. Then, a few weeks ago, Roy got very sick. He ended up in the hospital, unconscious. Some of his kin, who feared he might die, wanted him baptized, wanted to know if I would do that. I was deeply touched and utterly confused.

"When?" I asked them, exploring the possibility of a stall.

"Soon." "Today." "In a few hours."

That's when the turbulence began for me—questions, confusions, fears, the what-if-he-dies? tempest, tornado, swirl of events happening too fast, too furious.

But now, weeks later—in the aftermath—I see what they wanted, no matter what words they were using. They wanted to bring a blessing upon him. By that, I mean that they wanted and needed—as all of us do—a sign. A sign that the cosmos, for all its cruelty and terror, contains more; that it is also, beyond the reaches of our understanding, flecked with some kind of beauty and intrinsic grace.

These intense times in our lives—these tornadoes, these bonfires—force us to stare into much that seems both mysterious and dangerous. We see all too clearly, at such times, the Mystery in all its power and force. We see its capacity to obliterate life as we know it, to create chaos, to destroy sentimentality or naivete, to snatch people away from us.

Blessings, at such times, have a power of their own—not, at their best, a power to diminish what we are experiencing or to tame it or hide it or make it go away, but a power to add something to it, some sense of the possibility that the Mystery is even more than terrifying, that it is also, in some sense, magnificent. And endurable, something we are capable of being in relationship with, something we may choose, at times, even to celebrate, to stand in the midst of, singing out holy.

We speak of blessings, often without paying much attention. "That was a mixed blessing," we say, meaning that it brought us good and bad tangled together. Or, "You better believe it; that was a blessing in disguise!" meaning that something rendered more than we thought it would. Or sometimes we say, "Bless his heart" or "Bless her heart," meaning that we appreciate someone deeply. Or if we hit our finger with a hammer, "God bless it!"

Blessings. Signs that the cosmos is more than terrifying, or chaotic—or both.

Theologian Howard Thurman tells of his son being afraid at night: "But Daddy, it's so dark in here, I'm scared! Something will hurt me, something will get me!" Terror spins him round like a tornado, burning like a bonfire in his imagination.

"Believe me, son, God is already in the room with you, and will look over you. I promise."

"Daddy, couldn't you please just ask God to put some skin on, then?"

That's the problem. God—whatever God may or may not be—has no skin on. There is so much that we cannot see, cannot understand, so much that baffles, confuses, frightens. William James framed it another way. Human beings, he commented once, sit amidst the mysteries of the cosmos like dogs and cats sitting in the family library.

To get the full impact of that, you have to imagine one of those old and elegant libraries, such as would have existed in certain homes during James's time. Imagine rows and rows of volumes—the classics—each containing whole worlds, altogether millions of words of wisdom and understanding, depth, and richness, packed into row upon row, in tall, wobbling stacks.

To be a dog or cat in such a place, to be in the midst of all of it, present to all of it, entirely close to it, but discerning so little of its real meaning . . . There stand we before the stars, wagging our tails, and wondering. And sometimes, from that perspective, things look chaotic, or unholy, or terrifying.

Blessings are but the signs we receive, from one another or from circumstance alone, that there is more to it than that and that we do indeed belong right in the midst of it. That's why they asked me, "Could you baptize him? Could you put the water of life upon his burning forehead, that we might for a time gather around him and remember his preciousness together, remember what we do know, what we are sure of, which is that we love him?

At the Minnesota State Fair in 1982— it was a very hot day— my husband Tom's cherry snowcone fell from its paper cup and landed smack on our infant son's head, down below in a stroller. Plunk! A frightened wail, then a grin—a sense of coolness and sweetness as this lovely and unexpected crimson syrup ran down his cheeks and to his mouth, as crushed ice settled round his hot little neck.

"Ah! Blessings from the cosmos!" his grin seemed to be saying. "I've been blessed, been baptized by a snowcone! And here all along I had thought life nothing more than an unholy burning desert full of pig barns, Ferris wheels, and merry-go-rounds. But now this, this coolness, this sweetness, this joy! What is the meaning of this?"

Could it be that we do indeed walk sightless among miracles? That we might be the intended recipients of untold blessings? I know the counter-argument: we may be walking sightless, sister, but show me that it's among miracles. Reason tells me that life is basically nasty, brutish, and short.

Show me that we're not walking among miracles. Take your furry paw, pull down the library book that tells me so, and put it in my furry paw. Show me that there is no grace or beauty, however hidden, in this bright darkness where God has no skin, this hospital bed, this snow cone, this storm-tossed boat.

Our reason can take us far—perhaps farther than our other faculties—but even our reason doesn't take us far enough. We yearn still for blessings, signs that the cosmos is more than terrifying and unholy, kindnesses, gestures of compassion, bits of good luck, unexpected breakthroughs, sustaining words.

It isn't a real blessing if it reduces and simplifies. It is real only if it refuses to do that and instead magnifies and incites, invites us into our own wholeness and capacity. It is true blessing only if it increases our ability to stand together in the thunderstorm, arms up, singing out holy.

Blessing—a sign, a concrete sign, that somehow, despite life's disastrousness, there just may be a cherry snowcone aimed smack at your neck, too. That's what Jesus meant, I think. What he was witnessing to, in those words that he spoke when the turbulent boat ride had ended.

"No, listen," he was saying. "It isn't just that those who do the best, get the best. The poor are blessed too. And the doubtful. And blessed are you when you're laughing, or weeping. Blessed. Just to be alive is to deserve blessing. You are beloved, and you have a place here."

Ironic. Nowadays the guys who have been through rough boat rides don't necessarily do the blessings. Instead, the priests— the ordained ones—are supposed to do the blessings, to be the givers of the sign, the holders of the wine and the bread, the holy water, as though a skinless God could ever be contained in such narrow places, as though a universe as stunning as this, as dazzling and dangerous, would ever allow Itself to be so confined.

I, an ordained one, know better. Do you know that I feel much more blessed than blessing when I come here? You bless me. This place blesses me. All the time.

And this place, this place where blessing happens, which seems so strong and safe and broad-raftered, has burnt before. And still, in other places, other churches are burning. And I wonder, are blessings happening in the midst of those blazes, somehow? Is there power—does someone have power, do we have power—to give a sign, make a sign for anyone at all, that there is more to all of this than just terror?

When the children from those burnt churches go to bed at night and lie in the dark, remembering what their church school rooms looked like afterwards—the soggy, fire-hosed walls and buckled windows—when they lie in bed, afraid, does someone find words to speak to them that help them know that they are holy, and blessed? That God may not have skin but does have compassion—and for them?

When the cosmos turns tempestuous, do we have the power to give each other blessings? To be givers of the sign?

If not, then who can?

Maybe it was a crazy kind of faith leap, but I took it anyway. Like a dog in a library, furry-pawed, and tired of dozing, I just did it, went there, put the water on my sweet Roy's head, said it as best I could, however crudely.

"I baptize you in the name of the Almighty God who created you, in the name of Jesus whose life showed you all you need to know about coming to the other side of the storm, and in the name of the Holy Spirit of Life, which guides and sustains always."

And what I meant was, "All right, you rascally rascal, you won, you got what you wanted. I'll do what I can to help you see how blessed you are, how beloved, to help you trust that the world, for all its pain and terror, still makes room for your preciousness. You've been such a giver of signs yourself—all those children, all those sandwiches, all those hugs and songs on the guitar. Now, my turn. Let me give you a sign."

I just did it, hand to forehead, wet with the water. Can't tell you how blessed I felt right then, touching Roy, standing in the storm with him, singing out holy.

—June 30, 1996

Sources

Adams, James Luther. *The Prophethood of All Believers.* Boston: Beacon Press, 1986.

Alinsky, Saul D. *Reveille for Radicals.* New York: Vintage Books, 1989 (first edition University of Chicago Press, 1946).

——. *Rules for Radicals: A Practical Primer for Realistic Radicals.* New York: Vintage Books, 1989.

Allen, Woody. *Without Feathers.* New York: Random House, 1975.

BeFriender Ministry Training Manual, revised edition. St. Paul, Minnesota: The Saint Paul Seminary, School of Divinity, University of St. Thomas, 1994.

Biblical passages from the King James Version.

Conroy, Pat. *The Prince of Tides.* Boston: Houghton Mifflin, 1986.

Dickens, Charles. *A Christmas Carol.* New York: Franklin Watts, 1969.

Eisler, Riane. *Sacred Pleasure: Sex, Myth and the Politics of the Body—New Paths of Power and Love.* San Francisco: Harper Collins, 1995.

Eliot, T. S. Reading #685 in *Singing the Living Tradition.* Boston: Beacon Press, 1993.

Fahs, Sophia Lyon, and Dorothy T. Spoerl. *Beginnings: Earth, Sky, Life, Death.* Boston: Starr King Press, 1958. For children.

Frankl, Viktor E. *Man's Search For Meaning.* New York: Simon and Schuster, 1984.

Hamilton, Edith. *Mythology: Timeless Tales of Gods and Heroes.* New York: New American Library, 1963 (20th printing, many printings since then).

Kretzmann, John P., and John L. McKnight. *Building Communities from the Inside Out: A Path toward Finding and Mobilizing a Community's Assets.* Evanston, Illinois: Center for Urban Affairs and Policy Research, Northwestern University, 1993.

Newhouse, Brian. *A Cyclist's Journey Home.* New York: Simon and Schuster, 1998.

"Now Light Is Less," Hymn #54 in *Singing the Living Tradition.* Boston: Beacon Press, 1993. Words by Theodore Roethke; music by Alfred Morton Smith.

Prechtel, Martín. *Secrets of the Talking Jaguar: A Mayan Shaman's Journey to the Heart of the Indigenous Soul.* New York: Jeremy P. Tarcher/Putnam, 1998.

Robbins, Wallace. Responsive Reading #460, "A Liberal Church," in *Hymns for the Celebration of Life.* Boston: Beacon Press, 1959.

Roberts, Elizabeth, and Elias Amidon, eds. *Earth Prayers from Around the World.* San Francisco: HarperCollins, 1991.

Shelley, Percy Bysshe. "Prometheus Unbound" in *The Complete Poetical Works of Shelley.* Cambridge, Massachusetts: Houghton Mifflin, 1901.

Shippee, John. "Harvester of Light" in *A Harvest of Light: Photographs by David Shippee,* B. Warner Shippee, Elizabeth P. Shippee, and Margit Long Donhowe, comps. St. Paul, Minnesota: Privately printed, 1998.

Thompson, G. F. *Slow Miracles.* San Diego: LuraMedia, 1995.

Thurman, Howard. *Disciplines of the Spirit.* Richmond, Indiana: Friends United Press, 1997.

Trumbauer, Jean Morris. *Sharing the Ministry: A Practical Guide for Transforming Volunteers into Ministers.* Minneapolis: Augsburg Fortress, 1995.

Wieman, Henry Nelson. *Man's Ultimate Commitment.* Carbondale, Illinois: Southern University Press, 1958.

Zoss, Joel, and John Bowman. *Diamonds in the Rough: The Untold History of Baseball.* New York: Macmillan, *1989.*